Essay Becomes Easy

Part I

Analysis * Persuasive * Classification * Evaluation
Reflective * Narrative * Compare and Contrast Essays

By EssayShark

Copyright Page

Table of Contents

Introduction

Five minutes have passed already and you are still looking at a blank sheet on your screen. "That's ok," you think, "I have enough time." You continue looking at the blank page. The next five minutes pass as one second. "Don't panic," says your internal voice calmly, "the most important thing is to start." Another half an hour passes away. "I don't know how to start! I won't ever complete this stupid essay." You finally lose your temper and are nearly screaming from despair.

If this happens to you now and then when you start working on essays, you should know one secret. While studying in high school, you need to write many essays. While studying at college, you need to complete essays. When you are a university student, guess what is the most popular type of assignment? That's right, the essay. So, here is the secret: essays are everywhere and the only way to cope with them easily is to practice.

Our book will act as a brilliant assistant for you in your trying hours. When you are looking for useful tutorials on the Web, you usually find only fragments of information that you need on writing essays. In our book, you will find everything that you need to know about certain types of essays, starting from structure and finishing with a checklist.

"Essay Becomes Easy. Part I" is not the kind of book that you read and click "delete" once you've finished. No way! As soon as you use it the first time, you'll move it to the most frequently opened folder and save it at least until you finish your studying! Enjoy writing essays with *"Essay Becomes Easy. Part I."*

Chapter 1. Analysis Essay Writing Guide

Amazing! You have just finished reading a book, reviewing a scholarly article, or watching a movie for your university. Such assignments are the greatest pleasure for students like you, as they switch the focus from routine college life to the topics of your interest, right? However, the book or article was definitely read for a reason, as your teacher asked you to write an analysis essay! Even if a single thought about these two words elevates your heart rate and puts you out of tempo, there is no place for fear. These easy-to-follow tips will help you on your challenging academic path when writing an analysis essay, and will help make it perfectly great!

What's So Special About the Analysis Essay?

If the word combination "analysis essay" sounds foreign to you, keep calm, because you have definitely written something similar before. An analysis essay is a type of academic paper that requires conveying a particular idea and defending it in a convincing manner. Students use analyzed sources as a basis for developing their arguments, examining and interpreting them in the most appropriate way. The primary academic challenge when writing an analysis essay is the importance of taking on a variety of positions, highlighting the "for" and "against" arguments and not necessarily drawing some powerful inferences. The primary purpose of an analysis essay is not to express your point of view or provide your reflection to the analyzed source, but to develop critical thinking and take on a higher analytical position. With the help of an analysis essay, you will provide sound, logical and unbiased feedback for each of the listed arguments without expressing personal reflections or defending at least one of the described points of view.

Professors often create challenging tasks for their students, proposing difficult topics for observation. For instance, your teacher may ask you to highlight the positive consequences of war, ignoring the deleterious effects of the war as a social disaster. Though writing on such topic may be exceedingly complicated, it will change the way your thinking is programmed. Before we start exploring the nuances of writing analytical essays, let's determine the main benefits you will receive after reviewing this guide:

- Ability to defend controversial arguments

- Selecting peer-reviewed sources independently

- Defending unpopular points of view

- Providing sound reasoning

- Facilitating your academic success

Are you ready to start?

Types of Analysis Essays

The classification of analytical essays depends on the object of analysis. Accordingly, we may distinguish the following types of analytical papers, providing essential recommendations towards working on them.

Literary work analysis. Read a literary masterpiece and analyze it, focusing on the emotions, situations, characters and choose a favorite quote and find its impact on the whole work.

Poetry analysis. Concentrate on the poem's structure, content, historical background, overall significance of the work and exclusivity of the author's style.

Character analysis. Focus not on the character's appearance or actions, but think about the character's development and transformation, if there is any. Take into account the character's mental reformation, personality traits, and behavioral model.

Process analysis. Describe the process of changing states through several stages; you may analyze different processes that interest you.

Causal analysis. Concentrate on the process and start asking yourself thousands of questions to find out the causes of the process; it is a WHY-analysis. Imagine yourself a four-year-old curious child trying to find the answers to questions like "Why the sky is blue?" and start writing this analytical paper.

Analysis Essay Writing Structure

The structure of all the academic papers is similar because it depends on certain standards of academic writing. Nevertheless, the content is significantly different, that is why it is worthy of dedicating several minutes to finding out the specifics of the analysis essay's content.

Introduction. This part of an analytical essay is used to present the argument and put the reader in the picture of the discussed topic. The writer should indicate the analyzed source, its title, general overview, and brief background information about the author or the source in general. For instance, if you analyze a play (let it be *A Raisin in the Sun*), you should accurately indicate the author (Lorraine Hansberry), the title, and general overview of the play. To make your overview laconic but informative, write about the complex nature of the problems developed in the play (racial discrimination, social inequality, wealth accumulation, etc.) and summarize these problems. You may develop each of them in body paragraphs, providing quotations to support your thoughts. Additionally, you should define the central idea of the analysis and write a convincing thesis statement that reflects the controversy of a research question. In a thesis statement, it is worthy to prove the significance of the analysis (it will draw the reader's attention!) and specify the key idea of analysis.

*Please note that, as an analysis essay requires dividing a general theme into narrow subcategories, it is important to divide your argument into several ideas which will further be proved in the main body of the analysis essay. For instance, you may identify three key points that will be further highlighted in the body paragraphs.

Main body. Each section in this part should be dedicated to a particular aspect of your thesis and provide a comprehensive evaluation of this issue. The following structure will help you to organize your thoughts logically.

Topic sentence. This is the starting point of your argument's development. This sentence should specify the main idea of the body paragraph and make a particular claim.

Analysis. Provide supporting evidence for your claim and evaluate it. This part of the paragraph should prove the author's credibility in a laconic manner (approximately two sentences).

Evidence. In this section of the paragraph, it is essential to establish connections between the main idea highlighted in the topic sentence and the evidence provided in the analysis part. Make sure that your evidence is comprehensive enough and entirely supports your idea.

Concluding sentence. Here it is worthy to restate the fundamental idea of the argument, explain its significance to the topic of research and relation to the analysis in general.

You may write as many body paragraphs as you can, but writing more is not equal to writing better. In this way, write as much as your thesis statement requires. If your thesis statement consists of three ideas, dedicate a paragraph to each of them and write three body paragraphs. Following this model, you will receive a standard 5-paragraph essay!

Conclusion. This part of an analysis essay has the highest research value! For making your conclusion powerful, break it into three sections.

1. Restate the thesis statement and connect it with the topic discussed.

2. Summarize the key ideas from the thesis statement and provide overview of the analysis.

3. Write a concluding sentence explaining the significance of the study. You may include brief information about the lessons taken from this research. It will be a final accord both for you and your audience, signalizing your comprehensive approach to carrying out profound academic research and making a systematic analysis.

Stages of Writing an Analysis Essay

Following these steps will help you not to miss anything on the way of creating an irresistible analytical paper.

1. Choose a subject of interest and narrow it down to the particular topic of your analysis. Establish the purpose of writing, taking into account the requirements of a potential target audience and the questions you want to answer during the investigation.

2. Develop your own opinion about the selected topic. Yes, it's that important! Your position will be declared in the analysis essay, as it will be influencing the decision-making and the conclusions during your analysis.

3. Dedicate some time for materials search and selection. Collect the supplementary literature relevant to your topic and investigate it. Read and analyze the chosen material, noticing the key ideas and the opposing views. Choose the ideas which coincide with your opinion and those that counter your argument completely.

4. Establish connections between the opposing views and choose the key ideas to be highlighted in your analysis. Write down the summary of these points (it will create a frame for your analytical paper!). Make sure your understanding of summarized ideas is clear and their

interpretation is logical. Create an outline of your future analysis essay. It may look like the following example:

Analytical Paper Outline

I. Introduction

    A. Attention-grabber

    B. Information about analyzed source (author, title, context)

    C. Brief background information

    D. Thesis statement

II. Body paragraphs

    A. Topic sentence

    B. Evidence (quote or theoretical frame)

    C. Analysis of the quotation

    D. Concluding sentence

III. Conclusion

    A. Restating the thesis statement

    B. Summarizing the arguments and extending them

    C. Proving the significance of analysis

    D. Concluding sentence

5. Tighten your argument! After exploring the opposing ideas and analyzing and establishing connections between them, it is the high time for developing a controversial argument that will serve as a central problem of your research — a thesis statement!

Advice on Writing a Powerful Analytical Thesis Statement

Make it structural! The prior purpose of each analysis is to break a complicated idea into simpler elements and evaluate them for drawing some inferences. An analytical thesis statement should do the same — divide one idea into several components for their further development in the body paragraphs.

Make it specific! It should be neither too broad nor too narrow — just about one or two sentences explaining the main problem of the paper.

Make it controversial! A thesis statement should reflect your interest in research, proving the significance of the analysis. Secret tip: fill your thesis statement with a conflict that will be solved in the concluding part of the essay. It will attract your reader and make your article more scientifically valuable!

In this way, your thesis statement should be a laconic formulation of the problem with a clear structure and a controversial opinion. If it sounds too complicated, check the following example and try to make something similar:

An analysis of the modern marketing industry shows its increasing influence on society, creating a challenge of choice for the modern people: letting the consumerism progress and improve the economy or saving the children from materialistic values.

1) It's high time for the first draft! Writing the draft is a must for building up a proper, well-defined structure for your essay and linking the ideas in the logical order.

2) Write an introduction and specify the object of analysis, narrowing the topic sentence by sentence.

3) Write the body paragraphs about the ideas presented in your thesis statement. Don't forget to support these ideas with quotes or examples from peer-reviewed sources.

4) Summarize the arguments in the conclusion and restate the main points from the introductory part. Do not include any new information in the concluding sentence.

5) Go through the whole paper once again. Check whether the key points in the thesis statement and conclusion correlate with each other. Analyze the structure and development of the arguments in your essay. Kindly check the paper for plagiarism, grammar, and spelling mistakes.

Guidelines and Tightening Your Essay

The most important question that enters students' minds before writing is, of course, the selection of a topic. Here are some examples of successfully chosen themes for effective analysis essays.

1. Human phobias and roots of their origins.

2. Ecological crisis in a globalized world.

3. Historical influence on the change of gender roles.

4. Influence of marketing on children, teenagers or adolescents.

5. Well-being in nuclear and extended families.

6. The impact of the Internet on recruiting and workforce flow.

7. Ethical issues in business, sports or management.

8. National identity in a multicultural world.

9. Portraying Scrooge in Dickens' *The Christmas Carol*.

10. Medea as an ideal of a tragic hero.

11. Differences between a book and the movie based on it.

12. Communication differences between males and females.

13. The role of national, religious or cultural stereotypes in the modern world.

14. Visual analysis of persuasive details in advertisement.

15. Virgil's role in *The Divine Comedy*.

Enhancing Your Title

Remember that the working title of the paper is almost a quarter of an essay's success, so do not give your academic papers titles like "Ecological Crisis," "National Stereotypes" or "Ethical Issues," because such headings are too general — they neither specify the subject of the paper, nor show the main problem of your work. Try to make your titles comprehensive — specify whom, where, when and for what purposes do you investigate. However, remember that a successful title should not exceed 12 words, even if it is your course paper, so make your titles short but attention-grabbing!

Choosing the Appropriate Analysis Strategy

Depending on the topic you choose, you may also select the most effective analytical approach for improving the quality of your essay.

Established theory as a basis for analysis. For supplementing your analysis with a theoretical framework, choose a particular philosophical, religious or psychological theory and establish connections between this theory and analyzed source. For instance, imagine that you need to write an analytical paper about the philosophy of religion and existence of God. However, covering this topic without reference to the authorities of philosophical thought is merely impossible, isn't it? Accordingly, you may try to explore the ideas of Nietzsche and Epicurus and compare them to make your essay more persuasive and valuable.

Analyzing the arguments of the source. If your primary task is to go through the arguments developed by the author and critically evaluate them, you should highlight the main differences between these arguments, identify their strong and weak points, and provide a balanced, unbiased overview of these arguments without supporting any of them.

Rhetorical analysis. In this type of analysis, your prior task is to concentrate on the text, the use of rhetorical strategies and the author's professionalism. To do this, you should read the text several times consciously, identify the rhetorical devices, and find out whether their usage is persuasive enough. Do not forget about the TRACE rule "Text, Reader, Author, Context, and Exigence" and establish connections between all of these elements.

Deconstruction approach. This type of analysis is oriented on destroying the traditional points of view through critical evaluation of the source. Indeed, deconstruction represents the rebuilding of the source, dividing it into a variety of fragments and analyzing each of these elements. This approach helps to find the small details which make up the whole. The representative example of deconstructive analysis is looking for the conflicts, contradictions, multiple meanings and errors in the books with brilliant reputations. For instance, you may analyze the weak points of Gatsby as a character in Fitzgerald's *The Great Gatsby* to destroy the popular thoughts and suggest a non-standard analysis of the plot.

Mistakes to Avoid While Analysis Essay Writing

Even the students with brilliant writing skills encounter challenges when structuring their essays according to the demands of academic style; that is why it is worthy to check your paper for the following commonly made mistakes:

1. **Including a thesis statement in one of the body paragraphs.** A thesis statement should be put into the last sentence of the introduction.

2. **Making the essay longer with the help of unnecessary statements.** Let each sentence be valuable and perform its informative or persuasive function, as academic writing highly appreciates the quality of the papers, and not the number of words.

3. **Incorrect use of quotes.** Using quotations is an excellent tool for supporting your arguments. However, using them in the introductory paragraph or conclusion will not be appropriate for academic writing.

4. **Including new arguments in the conclusion.** If you have one more argument to write about, include it into body paragraph and provide supporting evidence for developing this idea.

5. **Using ordinary language instead of academic.** Do not use colloquial style in an analytical essay, as it may weaken your arguments and decrease the quality of your writing.

6. **Incorrect spelling, punctuation or grammar.** Receiving an A+ for an essay with at least minor grammar mistakes is impossible, which is why it is critically important to proofread each sentence and make changes if needed.

7. **Copyright infringement is out of the question.** Do not forget to check your analytical essay for plagiarism to avoid accusations of academic misconduct.

Analysis Essay Writing Checklist

Introduction

- Have you comprehensively indicated the source, topic or issue you are analyzing?

- Did you define the central idea and purpose of this research?

- Have you developed a working thesis statement and put it into the last sentence of your introduction?

- Does your thesis statement consist of several ideas which will be further developed in body paragraphs?

- Does your introduction invite the reader's attention to the analyzed issue?

Body

- Does each paragraph highlight a particular idea from your thesis statement?

- Is the structure of each paragraph logical and clear (topic sentence → analysis → evidence → conclusion)?

- Does the number of your body paragraphs coincide with the number of ideas presented in the thesis statement?

- Have you used quotations and arguments from reputable sources to support your ideas and provide evidence?

- Have you developed your arguments in the most convenient way?

Conclusion

- Have you restated the thesis statement and connected it with the central idea of the analysis?

- Have you provided an overview of the analysis and summary of the arguments?

- Have you written the powerful concluding sentence proving the importance of your study?

- Have you achieved your purpose indicated in the introductory part?

- Are you satisfied with the results of your analysis in general?

Works Cited

Eiselein, Gregory. "Deconstructive Analysis." k-state.edu. N.p., 2006. Accessed 14 Jan. 2017.

"Four Types of Essay: Expository, Persuasive, Analytical, Argumentative." *Access-socialstudies*.

    N.p., 2008. Accessed 14 Jan. 2017.

"How to Write an Analytical Essay: Example, Topics, Outline." *Essay Writing with EssayPro*. N.p.,

    2015. Accessed 14 Jan. 2017.

"How to Write an Analysis Essay*." AnswerShark.com*. https://answershark.com/writing/essay-

    writing/analysis-essay/how-to-write-analysis-essay.html. Accessed 14 Jan. 2017.

Jewell, Richard. *Advanced Methods of Analysis*. Tc.umn.edu. N.p., 2012. Accessed 14 Jan. 2017.

Kearney, Virginia. "How to Write a Summary, Analysis, and Response Essay Paper With

    Examples." *LetterPile.com*. N.p., 2016. Accessed 14 Jan. 2017.

Kearney, Virginia. "50 Critical Analysis Paper Topics." *LetterPile.com*. N.p., 2016. Accessed 14

    Jan.2017.

Tardiff, Elyssa and Allen Brizee. "Tips and Examples for Writing Thesis Statements." *Purdue*

    Online Writing Lab, Owl.english.purdue.edu. N.p., 2014. Accessed 14 Jan. 2017.

"Writing an Analysis Essay." *AcademicHelp*, AcademicHelp.net. N.p., 2012. Accessed 14 Jan.

    2017.

Sample 1. What Are the Chemical Causes of Falling in Love?

Falling in love is often described as one of the brightest experiences in human existence. Nevertheless, there is still no final scientific answer to the questions like why and how an individual becomes enamored with someone else. Some studies suggest that these are the hormonal changes that cause the sensation of falling in love, while others suggest that this altered mental state is induced by a change of serotonin transporter density. One fact is clear, though: the psychological state of being in love reflects in many physiological processes.

A study conducted by Marazziti and Canale compared the hormonal levels of people in the early stages of romantic relationships and those who were single or in longterm relationships (931-936). The results of the investigation show that people newly fallen in love have significantly higher cortisol levels in comparison to the control group. This change reflects the stress that they face during the establishment of the new social contact. Besides the testosterone levels are also reported to be influenced by falling in love. Men, who have been recently engaged in a romantic relationship demonstrated notably lower testosterone levels than the individuals from the control group. With significantly higher levels of testosterone, women who had fallen in love showed the opposite results. Marazziti and Canale interpret it as if new emotional bonds at the early stage of a relationship temporarily eliminate some dissimilarities between sexes, making women more masculine and men more feminine. Men from the first group also had a lower level of follicle-stimulating hormone (FSH). At the same time, the levels of luteinizing hormone (LH), progesterone, estradiol, dehydroepiandrosterone sulfate (DHEAS) and androstenedione were within normal limits among both first and second groups, showing no noticeable differences between them.

It is remarkable that all these hormonal changes were state-dependent and reversible. The repeated hormone level measurements after 12-18 months showed no noticeable difference between individuals from the first group, some of whom were still in the same relationship, and from the second one. Such outcome means that all described hormonal changes are typical only for the early stages of the romantic relationship and decrease with time.

Another study has found that it is the change of the platelet serotonin transporter that is responsible for many visible effects of falling in love, such as, for example, intrusive thoughts about the partner (Marazziti et al. 741-745). People who are at the early stages of the romantic relationship are often compared to individuals with obsessive-compulsive disorder (OCD) because of their obsession with another person. According to this investigation, there is a biological explanation underlying this anecdotal observation. The scientists compared the levels of the 5-HT serotonin transporter between three groups: those who have recently fallen in love, unmedicated patients with OCD, and a control group of single individuals without mental disorders. The investigation has ascertained that the density of the platelet serotonin transporter was noticeably lower among the people from the first and the second groups in comparison to the control group. The result shows that falling in love interfaces with neurochemical changes, which involves the functioning of the 5-HT transporter. These changes are similar to those experienced by people with OCD.

As we see, love is not only psychological, but also a physiological condition which is characterized by some biochemical patterns. There are different points of view concerning the mechanisms which cause people to fall in love. After examining the results of few studies devoted to this question, the conclusion can be made that emotion felt at the early stages of the romantic relationship is induced by both changes in the level of hormones (such as testosterone, cortisol, and FSH) and in the density of the serotonin 5-HT transporter.

Works Cited

Marazziti, D. et al. *Alteration of the Platelet Serotonin Transporter in Romantic Love.*

Psychological Medicine 29.3 (1999): 741745. https://www.ncbi.nlm.nih.gov/pub

med/10405096.

Marazziti, Donatella and Domenico Canale. "Hormonal Changes When Falling in Love."

Psychoneuroendocrinology 29.7 (2004): 931-936. https://www.ncbi.nlm.nih.go

/pubmed/15177709.

Sample 2. An Analysis on the Effects of Gambling

In today's world, people are more incline to try something extraordinary, to receive a new dose of adrenaline. There are many ways of getting it and sometimes they turn out to be harmful to all the aspects of our lives. People are obsessed with the idea of becoming rich and having all the money they can. It results in the desire to find the easiest and quickest way of becoming wealthy, namely they fall into gambling. They become addicted and it ruins their families, friendships, and takes away their career prospects. Without a doubt, people are addicted because of the mentioned set of reasons and very often they do not manage to explain them.

People who start gambling do not presuppose they become addicted step by step. The point is that gambling makes them suffer psychologically, and they lose their families, all of their possessions and in general, lose themselves — their lives. People become addicted because they believe they can keep an eye on the chance, that is they see only the illusion of the possibility to have control over the gambling. Moreover, it happens when they are lucky to win one time and they are convinced this luck will always be next to them. Nobody can be confident in victory and it does not matter how many skills and abilities a person may have.

Another point is that it is human nature to remember wins more than losses. It is easy to think that, because a great deal of money was won once, success in gambling is a certainty, and next time, even more money will be won. The problem is that the idea of easy money leads to addiction and there is no way out. This luck makes the gambler sure they are really good at that game and only encourages them to continue playing.

What should be mentioned is that not all the people are equally vulnerable to become addicted to gambling. Not everybody has the same immunity to stay away from gambling and even if trying once they have the will to quit. People who are at a great risk suffer loneliness or depression and see gambling as the only way to hide from the world in the illusion of wealth and luck. What is more, some people are likely to become addicted to running away from life's problems, to forget about some emotional and physical pain. Still, the research has shown that gambling is a psychological disease and those who feel they are keen on impulsive behaviour, risk and excitement should not even try. "In California, about 10% of adults aged 18 and over — 2,900,000 people (based on the 2013 California population estimate) — are 'at-risk' of becoming problem gamblers at some time in their lives. They are generally people that gamble often and consider it to be their main or preferred form of entertainment, but do not put gambling before family or work"(calpg.org). Some people support the idea that those who become addicted to gambling are weak and are lacking self-confidence, while others are convinced that addicted individuals are not able to control their desire and they need professional help.

To sum up, gambling can ruin a person's life and very often we risk to lose more valuable things than money. So before starting, everyone should think whether it is worth doing it.

Works Cited

"Why Do People Become Addicted?" *Jeu-Aidereference.Qc.ca*, 2016, http://www.jeu-aidereference.qc.ca/www/why_people_become_addicted_en.asp?cmpt=2.

"Stages of Gambling."*California Council on Problem Gambling*, 2016, http://www.calpg.org/stages-of-gambling-2/.

Chapter 2. Persuasive Essay Writing Guide

Do you have difficulties with persuading people to accept or even adopt your point of view? It is high time to say final goodbyes to such problems and explore the art of building powerful arguments.

What's So Special About Persuasive Essay Writing?

A persuasive essay is a type of academic paper that requires taking a particular position (for or against the issue) and building a set of arguments to convince the reader. To write this paper effectively, you may imagine yourself a lawyer defending a case before a jury.

In a persuasive essay, your prior objective is not only to convince the audience using arguments or reason, but also to encourage the reader to take on your point of view or take some action. You can achieve this purpose with the help of factual supporting evidence, logical structure, and proper conclusions. A good persuasive essay explains not only why your position is correct, but also why the opposite idea is incorrect. To build the connections between your thoughts and the opposing views, you should carry out prolific research, get a clear vision of both sides of the issue, and explain everything in a logical, well-structured written manner.

Do not be afraid of building weak arguments or providing non-convincing evidence. Persuasive writing is the main tool of modern blogging, marketing, politics, and other spheres. Just look around and create something better!

Before We Start: Let's Exercise a Little Bit

1. Choose your point of view. For being maximally persuasive, it is essential to choose the position you'll enjoy defending. Develop the purpose of your writing. Consider the solutions you will be offering as a way out of the problem highlighted in the essay.

2. Create an image of your audience. Imagine the people you will be trying to convince. Consider whether or not your audience agrees with your position and why.

3. Carry out extensive research. A persuasive essay will not perform its main function successfully without providing logical supporting evidence. Due to this, you should expand the horizon of your own experience and knowledge. Choose peer-reviewed literature, interview the experts, and peruse the library and find what you need!

4. Think on the structure of your future essay. Choosing the most appropriate order for highlighting your arguments is critically important. Figure out which arguments are convincing enough and develop your own convincing strategy.

5. Convince the audience! To do it effectively, use a wide range of examples, refer to experts' thoughts, provide logical reasons, state facts, and develop irresistible arguments using your enthusiasm and profound knowledge.

Persuasive Essay Writing Structure

According to the norms of academic writing, the persuasive essay, just like any other, must contain an introduction, main body, and conclusion. However, it is better to concentrate not on "how" but "what" to write when planning your persuasive essay. Developing the arguments effectively may become a real challenge for students, especially for those not having background knowledge about the most appropriate structure for this type of academic writing.

Introduction. This is just a little part of your paper that helps readers determine whether the whole paper is interesting or not. Try to make it informative, attention-grabbing, and even a bit controversial. To make your introduction perfect, follow these steps:

- Use a "hook": it is the essential part of the introduction. The main function of the "hook" is to grab the reader's attention and invite him or her into the issue.

- Provide a background: expand the information provided in the "hook;" demonstrate your comprehensive knowledge of the topic in several sentences.

- Develop a thesis statement: write one or two sentences about the purpose of your paper, proving its significance. Do not forget to include your arguments into the thesis statement. Though these steps seem to be easy to follow, some students encounter many problems before writing, because they cannot find the most appropriate words for opening the essay (the "hook"). To eliminate this problem, here are several useful ideas for your opening:

1. Unusual detail: *Though the economy is continually developing and improving, it cannot provide humans with unlimited investments for the realization of their ideas.*

2. Strong statement: *It would not be an exaggeration to say that the modern age is the age of increased consumerism: people measure their life successes by money; which is why the quality of their life becomes dependent on the size of their capital.*

3. Quotation: *The function of education is to teach one to think intensively and to think critically. Intelligence plus character — that is the goal of true education* (Martin Luther King, Jr.).

4. Anecdote. Writing about misbehavior in the educational setting, you may use the following anecdote: *Mother: "Why are you home from school so early?" Son: "I was the only one who could answer a question." Mother: "Oh, really? What was the question?" Son: "Who threw the eraser at the principal?"*

5. Historical or statistical fact: *In the 90's, researchers indicated that society had returned to basic values, not caring about the price or brand, but looking at things' practicality, quality, and value.*

6. Question: *Industrial engineering encounters a real challenge today: how to provide people with modern interior and exterior decisions, improving the quality of life and saving money simultaneously?*

7. Outrageous statement or exaggeration: *The appearance of Gestalt psychology signaled a new way of treatment for psychological issues, as it modified the way of thinking for millions of people.*

Writing a successful opening is just the first step of making your essay structurally correct, readable, and effective. To keep up the good work, read the following steps and come up with the idea of an irresistible thesis statement.

- Specify the topic of your paper in a laconic manner.
- Impose reasonable limits on the suggested topic.
- Propose the structural organization of your paper (list the arguments).

Throughout the entirety of the thesis statement, you should prove your readers the following: *I've carried out prolific research, I know what I think about it, and I know how to prove I am right.*

Example of a thesis statement:

The problem of Maquiladoras in the US-Mexico Border region is exceedingly important, as its disastrous effects have more than local value: their severity deserves global attention, maintenance, and implementation of some effective solutions for overcoming the problem.

Now your thesis statement is great and your "hook" is impossible to be ignored. Let's move on to the content of the main body.

Main body. In this part of the paper, you should provide supporting evidence to maintain the opinion highlighted in your thesis statement. It should consist of at least three body paragraphs and provide logical reasoning to support your point of view. Referring to the example of the thesis statement given above, you may write a persuasive essay on the same topic, dedicating the first body paragraph to global attention for the problem of Maquiladoras. Write the second paragraph about the ways to encourage and maintain better circumstances, and the last — about the ways of implementing effective solutions and solving the problem.

Do not forget that you write a *persuasive* essay. This means that you will have to argue with the audience and prove your correctness with cogent reasons. As almost all issues surrounding humans can be evaluated from two different sides, the challenge of a good persuasive writer is to provide readers with both sides of the issue, anticipate the opposing views, and include counter-arguments into the main ideas of your essay. For instance, you may use one out of three body paragraphs to discuss the opposing opinions and provide counter-arguments.

To make the content of your body paragraphs exceedingly persuasive, use supporting evidence, because facts, quotes, statistics and examples together work miracles! Here are tips for writing body paragraphs.

1. Start from the topic sentence and use it as a tool for clarifying your position. Take one argument from your thesis, state it in the topic sentence and provide additional details if needed. Before

writing, think about your audience — find out what needs to be described and how you can achieve it. Example: *The families living near Maquiladoras do not have the opportunities for providing and maintaining a relatively satisfactory quality of life, saving money or buying luxurious items.*

2. Do not forget about concession statements! Concession statements are the opposing views which should be broadly used in your body paragraphs. Concessions won't make your arguments weaker. Instead, they will prove your comprehensive understanding of the issue and demonstrate your ability to write from all the perspectives. Ignoring the opposing views is impossible and intolerant, which is why it is worthy to use some commonly known ideas, break them into patterns, and find out which patterns seem to be improper. You may even start your body paragraph from a concession, referring to the idea of an expert and indicating that part of this idea is valid. Further, you may prove why the other part of that idea is incorrect, developing your argument and persuading your readers. Example: *Despite significant environmental damages, Maquiladoras brings some advantages, as it represents a reliable source of profit for world-known corporations, oriented on the production of color televisions, textile and clothes, refrigerators, toys, etc.*

3. Use transition words to organize the whole essay and establish contact with the reader (*first, second, nevertheless, however, eventually, consequently, therefore, still, thus, besides, notwithstanding that, furthermore,* etc.)

Conclusion. This element of the paper usually provides a summary of the most essential details of the argument and restates what the reader should believe in.

1. State your thesis statement once again.

2. Summarize the main ideas of your argument and briefly describe your position.

3. Write a personal reflection, call for action or comment. Use one of the following approaches to do it effectively:

Prediction. You may propose the potential results of the situation discussed. Use either narrative or cause and effect discussion.

"Without a system of reforms from governmental structures, the raise in wages is likely to be neither necessary nor effective."

Recommendation. You may stress the action or suggest your solution.

"The quality of human life should be protected; that is why officials must save the lives of the poor, provide help and assistance in workplace search, increase the minimum wages significantly, and invite social workers for changing the labor set of mind of the people surviving in the grip of poverty."

Question. You may close your essay with a question, letting the readers draw their own inferences and make predictions.

"Does the problem of the economic gap between wealthy and underdeveloped countries have the chance to be solved once and forever?"

Quotation. You may use a quotation with calling for an action, prediction or question. It will work in any type of the paper.

"What is the best color?" said Finn. "The color of childhood" (Lady Augusta Gregory).

Stages of Writing a Persuasive Essay

Let's switch the focus from theory to practice! Now check the following steps and practice your persuasive writing skills.

1. Dedicate your time for choosing a topic. The topic should be attractive, relevant, and maximally original. Writing on this topic should be a pleasure for you!

2. Brainstorm a little bit. You should carefully think about several ideas to write about. Additionally, you can create a plan of developing those ideas and choosing the most appropriate organization of your essay.

3. Find supplementary readings. Writing on the topic you're not knowledgeable about will not be persuasive, that is why it is critically important to carry out extensive academic research, select relevant, peer-reviewed sources, and then read them and choose the arguments to be used in your thesis statement.

4. Select the most convincing idea. Go through the arguments you chose for further analysis and find the most powerful idea. The same you should do with the most convincing opposing idea. Establish connections between your position and the counter-argument and start planning your essay.

5. Create an outline. Organize your evidence to develop the most successful persuasive strategy. Remember the typical structure of an argumentative essay includes five or six paragraphs, including the following points:

a. Introduction ("hook" + background information + thesis statement).

b. Body paragraphs (topic sentence + supporting evidence).

c. Paragraph with opposing view (concession statement + description of the view + counter-argument).

d. Conclusion (restating the thesis statement + brief summary of the paper + personal comment).

6. Write an introduction. Indicate precisely what you are writing about, not overwhelming the paragraph with unnecessary details. Put the subject of your research (thesis statement) into the last sentence of the introduction, following the ideas from the outline.

7. Body paragraphs. Start each paragraph with presenting one particular point of view. Use the evidence (quotes, examples, statistics) to support the arguments from the thesis. Write one or two paragraphs about the opposing ideas and use your arguments to refute it.

8. Conclusion. Use one of the elements of persuasive writing listed above (quotation, recommendation, question, prediction) and make your conclusion irresistible!

9. Revise your paper. In this phase, you should reorganize and modify your paper if it is necessary. Read your essay once again and consider whether it is persuasive enough. Concentrate on your thesis statement, the structure of building the arguments, and persuasiveness of the conclusion. All of these elements in combination transform your essay into a real masterpiece!

10. Proofread the paper and correct the mistakes. Do not forget about grammar, spelling or punctuation mistakes. Check your paper on plagiarism to make sure you that you have cited all of the sources properly.

Guidelines and Tightening Your Essay

A good topic of a persuasive essay should concentrate on a conflict of some sort. It is always better to talk about broadly discussed and most relevant "hot" topics — those that overwhelming the news, social media, and research databases. Surely, you may refer to the events of the past, re-evaluating the historical experience and suggesting an innovative point of view. Here are some of the most attractive points for a persuasive essay.

1. Does social media encourage loneliness?

2. Books vs. technology: who wins?

3. Mandatory school vaccinations: "for" and "against" arguments.

4. Should cities offer book crossing, bike sharing or public Wi-Fi?

5. Getting a license for becoming a parent: is it necessary?

6. Should advertisements be allowed in schools, public transport or television?

7. Do security cameras break privacy?

8. Is the concept of "American dream" currently important? If yes, is it attainable?

9. Making college education free: is it possible?

10. Are age-related stereotypes (age for marriage, driving age, voting age, drinking age) acceptable in modern society?

11. Should countries eliminate the geographical borders and welcome the immigrants?

12. Replacing student textbooks with tablets and notebook computers: causes and consequences.

13. Should colleges organize etiquette classes, dances and sports competitions?

14. Selling genetically modified foods under warning label: "for" and "against" arguments.

15. Should smokers pay a special type of tax for harm to their health?

As you can see, the majority of the topics are formulated as questions, as it is the most appropriate way of putting the conflict into your topic. Remember that choosing a controversial theme requires a title that is no less controversial! Due to this, it is necessary to make your headings attractive and informative, containing the core of the problem. So let your imagination run free and think up the most creative title for your persuasive paper!

Mistakes to Avoid While Writing a Persuasive Essay

This part is the last element of this guide that should be looked through before starting to write your essay, so make sure your understanding of all of the points listed below is clear. And, last but not least: it is better to prevent making mistakes than revise your paper several times, isn't it?

1. **Making your essay long, yet uninformative.** Writing about everything is not acceptable in persuasive papers, as you need to be precise, accurate and strict concerning the topic you discuss. Due to this, it is unnecessary to include several paragraphs of supplementary information in your essay, especially if this information is too broad or not related to the topic at all.

2. **Not caring about your audience.** Though you need to be laconic and precise, do not forget that your essay should be easy for comprehension, so provide explanations for particular terms or notions you use.

3. **Neglecting the paper structure.** Do not repeat the same arguments several times over, and make sure to use "step by step" principle when developing your ideas. Build your persuasive strategy thoroughly, imagining that each idea you defend is a brick — a small part that establishes a basis for the whole construction.

4. **Not using the supporting evidence.** Even if you believe that your words are entirely correct, support them with arguments from experts. It will transform an ordinary student paper into real scientific research and your words will make a lot more sense for the audience.

5. **Not paying attention to your style.** Consider the requirements of your audience and write in the appropriate tone. You may give your essay to a friend — it will help to identify sentences that are difficult to understand and paraphrase them.

Persuasive Essay Writing Checklist

After your research and writing work is done, use the following questions to check your paper and make final changes if needed.

Introduction

- Does your paper present a specific topic or issue for discussion?

- Does your topic contain a particular problem to be solved in the concluding part of the paper?

- Does your introduction open with an intriguing "hook" (unusual detail, exaggeration, strong statement, quotation, statistic, question or anecdote)?

- Have you provided brief background information on your topic in the introductory paragraph?

- Have you put an effective thesis statement into the last sentence of the introduction?

Body

- Does each paragraph in the main body highlight a single argument or idea?

- Does each body paragraph contain a topic sentence and supporting evidence (quotation, example, fact, statistics)?

- Is the structure of your body paragraphs built properly?

- Have you provided a paragraph with an opposing view?

- Have you presented and refuted the opposite view comprehensively?

- Have you used synonyms, terms with definitions or appropriate for academic style words?

- Have you used the transitional words to link the sentences and simplify the ideas?

- Is the structure of the sentences similar throughout the whole paper?

Conclusion

- Does your conclusion start from restating the thesis statement?

- Does your conclusion prove the correctness of your position and encourage the audience to act and think in the same way?

- Have you provided a personal reflection, comment, prediction or recommendation in the conclusion?

- Have you achieved your purpose, established before writing the paper?

Works Cited

"How to Write a Persuasive Essay." *AnswerShark.com*, https://answershark.com/writing/essay-writing/persuasive-essay/how-to-write-persuasive-essay.html.

"How to Write a Persuasive Essay." *Scribendi.com*, 2016, https://www.scribendi.com/advice/how_to_write_a_persuasive_essay.en.html.

Inez, Susan. "20 Persuasive Essay Topics to Help You Get Started." *Kibin.com*, 2015, https://www.kibin.com/essay-writing-blog/20-persuasive-essay-topics-help-get-started/.

"Tips on Writing a Persuasive Essay." *Time4writing*, 2016, http://www.time4writing.com/writing-resources/writing-resourcespersuasive-essay/.

"Writing the Persuasive Essay." *Waterford Union High School*, http://www2.waterforduhs.k12.wi.us/staffweb/sereno/mainpages/InfoLit/Microsoft%20Word%20-%20Writing%20the%20Persuasive%20Essay.pdf.

"101 Persuasive Essay and Speech Topics." *Ereading Worksheets*, http://www.ereadingworksheets.com/writing/persuasive-essay-topics/.

"60 Persuasive Essay and Speech Topics." *K12 Reader: Reading Instruction Resources*, http://www.k12reader.com/persuasive-essay-and-speech-topics/.

Sample 1: Evaluating the Cost of Space Exploration

In modern society, there are a large number of global questions which need to be considered. Space travel is one of the most significant parts of humanity, as well as one of the most innovative processes in the world. From these adventures, many everyday products were created, such as Teflon, the digital camera and GPS satellite navigation. This paper is aimed at the investigation of space exploration and the significance of it.

In fact, in the years of the Cold War, the space race had simple motives, such as the country's prestige and military superiority over the enemy. Both factors seem less important today when all countries are trying to work in space. However, it is unrealistic, especially without any great effort of patriotism and enormous costs, which requires space exploration. It is worth nothing to mention that this striving pay off many times over after occurring the space exploration by any country. Space travel requires more sophisticated circuits, fire-resistant paint, durable plastic, eternal adhesives and more. All over the world in order to implement this activity in life, millions of people work each year.

Thanks to space exploration over the past half-century, there have been more than 50,000 patents. Many essential inventions were created originally for space exploration, such as satellites, cell phones, and the common household Teflon pan. In the future, there will be created an enormous new sector of the world economy called "space tourism." However, most significantly, space technology will help in Earth's protection from the next Tunguska meteorite and help to resolve energy issues through the supply of thermonuclear fuel from the Moon.

In today's world, there is an incredibly large number of people who are involved with photography, and they use the digital camera. Nobody wants to mess around with film because everyone can use the digital format easily. It is cheaper and more convenient. Even Hollywood movies are shot with a digital camera. And here again is an achievement gained from space travel, because at the heart of digital cameras are CCD, so called from the light-sensitive photodiode chips based on silicon. They were first created in the 1960s. The crown of creation in this area was the orbital telescope Hubble, working for the benefit of science since 1991. Today's digital cameras, camcorders, digital TV and digital microscopes are widely used in medicine — the direct descendants of the cosmic photo technology.

Technology development is the primary purpose of spending money on space exploration. Hundreds of technological developments have moved from space to Earth and become a part of everyday life for millions of people. Also, scientific discoveries made with the help of space research allow us to increase our knowledge about the nature of the universe and advance fundamental science. Research from space travel can assist in resolving the energy problems of humankind. The space industry employs hundreds of thousands of people in many countries.

The direct development of the space program is space tourism, which over the years will become a major industry, providing employment to many people and bringing more profit. Space is inextricably linked to military technology, and in the future, it is possible to create space weapons, which will be many times greater than those existing today. For example, the kinetic weapons. An asteroid launched from its orbit on the path to Earth would be many times worse than any nuclear bomb (Launius et al. 1803). Just placing powerful space technology, it is possible to protect the planet from asteroids. Creating bases on the Moon and Mars will be the preparation of reserve shelters for humanity in case of disasters in the world. These colonies also save the planet from overpopulation, which is almost inevitable.

In conclusion, space is of a large political importance, success in extraterrestrial space raises the country's prestige. Space is a global objective, around which could unite all of the humanity forever forgetting the internal ethnic and religious feuds over time. Thus it can be said that spending money on space exploration is a great idea to achieve future accomplishments.

Works Cited

Launius, Roger D. et al. "Spaceflight: The Development of Science, Surveillance, and Commerce in

Space." *Proceedings of the IEEE*, vol 100, no. Special Centennial Issue, 2012, pp. 1785-1818.

Institute of Electrical and Electronics Engineers (IEEE), doi:10.1109/jproc.2012.2187143.

"The Business of Space Exploration, Business Daily – BBC World Service." *BBC*, 2016,

http://www.bbc.co.uk/programmes/p021y326. Accessed 9 Jan. 2017.

Sample 2. Persuasive Essay on Marriage

The world changes not even every minute, but every second, and it is hard to catch the moment of these changes. New technologies and industries continually develop, and more, people try modern techniques in education, social life, and politics. This way of progress influences all the principles and values that everybody follows afterward. In today's world, everything that was considered to be standard is transformed and nobody criticizes each other for some violation of the norm. One of the significant changes in modern society is that women do not feel the need to get married and create a family.

First of all, women today are very ambitious and concentrated on themselves. That means in recent decades, the female generation has become stronger and more confident in their abilities to be politicians and directors of successful companies, and they are ready to run their businesses. What is more, they realize they can manage to make a living on their own and there is no need for husbands who were earlier considered to be the main earners and supporters.

There were many stereotypes, and women could not do anything but care for their men and children, do laundry and make a dinner. "Research has shown that the 'marriage benefits' — the increases in health, wealth, and happiness that are often associated with the status — go disproportionately to men. Married men are better off than single men. Married women, on the other hand, are not better off than unmarried women" ("Is Marriage Worth The Trouble For Women?").Today they prove the opposite. Women feel they have enough skills and rights — that is, they can manage to feed themselves and to be totally independent.

One more point to support the idea is that, being in a marriage, women very often are tied with responsibilities, unable to do what they like, so they need to sacrifice free time to their hobbies and rest. "This is because the term 'wife' generally has a negative connotation. It usually means to basically be a domestic servant"("Marriage Today"). Having family, they are to act only in its interests and needs, and there is no place for personal pleasure. To be more precise, women see no point in marriage as it only takes away the opportunities for self-development. Nowadays, women are willing to try everything that life proposes, to travel around the world and to be free in their choices and preferences. They choose the way of living for themselves and enjoy the benefits it gives rather than sitting at home, cooking and waiting for the husbands to come home.

Still, some people do not like such a tendency and their opinion has a right to exist. The family is something that should always exist and without women, the family will not be full. Women are those who protect all the spiritual relationships between family members, she is a keeper of all the traditions and values. Moreover, many people are convinced that women have to be weaker than men and to obey them. Somebody has to show their superiority to keep the order in the society and it must be men. People think it is normal for women to set less perspective positions, to listen to men and to have the care of children and husband as their hobby. In addition, if there will not be families, there will be chaos in the community. In such a way, both generations will compete for the better place and the world will turn into a battleground, not a society where the marriage is a tool for everything sacred and connected with truth, love and support. Another point is that to be self-identified individuals, women do need the men. In marriage, they feel safe, have a wall to hide behind and a man who can solve all the problems and tackle all the difficulties women can not. "I am the head of this home so I can certain you and make sure that whatever you need you get it first before I get it"(Evans, "What a Woman Really Needs Today").

What is more, many women consider it to be a great possibility for self-development, namely traveling and career. The point is to be happy in your own way and it does not matter that if somebody is mot married they are not happy.

Works Cited

"What a Woman Really Needs — Marriagetoday." *Marriagetoday*, 2017,

http://marriagetoday.com/marriagehelp/what-a-woman-really-needs/.

"Is Marriage Worth the Trouble for Women?" *Psychology Today*, 2016,

https://www.psychologytoday.com/blog/insight-therapy/201510/is-marriage-worth-the-

trouble-women.

"Marriage Today." The Interactive Media Lab at the University of Florida, 2017,

http://iml.jou.ufl.edu/.

Chapter 3. Classification Essay Writing Guide

Don't you just enjoy when the name of paper is straightforward, and the instructions are clear? If yes, then writing a classification essay is for the students like you.

What's So Special about a Classification Essay?

A classification essay is a type of formal writing that requires organizing the subjects into different categories or groups using the same classification principle. This type of academic writing develops generalization and categorization skills of the author, establishing logical connections between the items and evaluating their shared characteristics.

When preparing to write a classification essay, you should focus on a particular broad subject and examine it for the elements that make it up. For instance, when you think about music, you may classify it by genre (rock, pop, jazz, electronic), mood (aggressive, fun, wistful, relaxing, intense), tempo (moderate, dynamic, lyric), etc. In this way, the primary objective of writing a proper classification essay is developing categorization skills and the ability to classify items based on a single criterion.

Classification essays exist to help you understand the topics that will be further discussed, that is why it is so important to collect more information about a particular theme and organize it accordingly. A good classification essay doesn't only sort the items into groups but also establishes logical connections between these items and rates them to a common standard. Thanks to writing a classification essay, you will:

- Obtain categorization and generalization skills

- Develop the structure of your writing

- Make your ideas logical and clear

- Facilitate your understanding of the topic

- Improve organization skill**s**

Tips on Writing an Effective Classification Essay

- **Identify the categories.** After the topic for your future essay is selected, divide it into groups and establish logical connections between elements. Try to be as thorough as you can, as leaving out an important category is entirely inappropriate for a good classification essay.

- **Sort by a single standard.** Once you have determined the categories, ascertain that they fit the single organizing criteria set. Organizing criteria are how you categorize the items into groups. Do not let an inappropriate principle destroy the logic of the paper. For instance, if your topic is *water sports* and classification principle is *tourist benefit*, you should not use any other unifying principle and write about extreme or dangerous sports.

- **Provide each group with examples equally.** Remember that you should write the same number of examples for each group. However, the biggest and the most critical group is usually reserved for last, so it might need a bit more detailed elaboration.

Classification vs. Division Essay

Students frequently misunderstand the primary purpose of a classification essay and write the papers which belong to other types of academic writing. For instance, writing a division essay instead of providing classification is the most common mistake. Let's find the difference to avoid these mistakes in your academic practice.

1. Purpose. A division essay breaks a particular topic into patterns for making the complicated issue more understandable. For instance, learning medicine is merely impossible without breaking the whole discipline into the specialties (neurology, psychiatry, and hematology). Due to this, the main purpose of writing a division essay is making a topic easier for comprehension through dividing it into smaller subtopics and investigating them. A classification essay does not only divide the subjects into smaller parts but also ranks the categories according to a particular principle or standard. In this way, a classification essay serves as a convenient way to arrange data and simplify decision-making, while a division essay exists for making the whole more understandable through its parts.

2. Mixing topics vs. mixing standards. In a division essay, it is necessary to establish appropriate categories and discuss them. For instance, imagine that you have to write a division essay about pollution. To investigate this topic deeply, you will have to divide it into at least three categories, writing about radioactive, biological, and chemical pollution from environmental hazards. In a classification essay, it is not essential just to divide the topic but rank or rate it to a common standard. When writing a classification essay about pollution, you will divide environmental hazards into biological, chemical, and radioactive, and investigate which of these

43

types is the most or the least dangerous. In this way, in a division essay, it is not allowed to mix topics, while in a classification essay you cannot mix standards — remember this point.

3. Problem. The most common problem of division essays is oversimplifying the topic. For instance, when students write that "Humans deal with loss in three ways: depression, compensation, and denial," they oversimplify the topic because assuming that all living beings cope with loss only in these three ways would not be correct. To rectify this mistake, you can say "Most humans deal with loss in three ways," which will establish certain limitations to your topic. In a classification essay, a commonly met problem is forgetting to write about exceptions for classification. For instance, if most humans deal with loss in the three listed ways, then there are people who find alternative ways of coping with stress, so they start exercising, eating healthy food, become engrossed in career, etc. These exceptions should necessarily be explained in each classification essay.

As you can see, the difference between division and classification is significant. Make sure you understand it clearly and don't mix up two different types of academic writing.

Classification Essay Writing Structure

The structure of a good classification essay should be built around the categories you write about, which is why it is essential to follow the following way of organizing your thoughts.

Introduction. Here you should clearly describe your topic and identify the group you are categorizing. If you have narrowed your topic or focused on a broader theme, you should indicate it from the very beginning. Also, feel free to include any informative or descriptive details in your introduction, but don't make them too long. Additionally, suggest the purpose of the essay and write an effective thesis statement for inviting the attention of the readers to your topic.

The thesis statement should be put in the last sentence of the introductory paragraph. As you write a very specific type of academic essay be sure to make your thesis statement maximally appropriate to the demands of a classification essay. Include the information about the topic and classification principle into your thesis statement. Feel free to name the categories if you wish and remember that your thesis statement should justify the specific groups chosen for classification. Here is an example: *Hawaiian tourists can enjoy many entertaining activities (topic), but some of the most popular are represented by three types of water sports (classification principle): sailing, snorkeling, and surfing (categories).*

Body paragraphs. Remember that each paragraph should open with a topic sentence that serves as a central element of the whole paragraph. Your topic sentence should narrow the focus of the entire essay to the category discussed in a particular paragraph. Here is an example: *Sailing in Hawaii is one tradition that has remained unchangeable over the years.* After your topic sentence is ready, maintain it by additional details and provide a more comprehensive illustration of the category.

You may structuralize your body paragraphs in any order, just make sure it is logical. For instance, you may start writing about the most common types of water sports and move to the least familiar. However, do not forget to establish logical connections between the categories. In this way, you may compare them, comment, summarize or augment some essential details, as a good classification essay does not only divide the subjects into groups but explores the connections between the groups and highlights them. Using comparisons and transitions will make the structure of the body paragraphs more smooth and easier for comprehension. Feel free to use the following transitional words, which are the most appropriate for usage in classification essay: firstly, subsequently, lastly, initially, in regard to, in terms of, the first kind (group, type), the second group (kind, type), the third type (group, kind), etc.

Conclusion. In the concluding paragraph, you have an opportunity to blend all the categories and approaches you have been investigating. You are free in structure for the closing paragraph. For instance, you may write about each type discussed in the essay again, summarize its strong and weak points, or you may emphasize the advantages of one category over the other and explain the reasons. One way or another, ascertain that your conclusion meets the purpose of the essay and conveys your main idea or inference properly.

Of course, you may experiment with the structure of your classification essay and develop ideas in the order you choose, but in any case, you should keep in mind the basic format suggested above and adhere to it. Briefly speaking, you should identify the topic in the introduction, present your classification principle in the thesis sentence, develop the topic and establish connections in the main body, and, finally, draw some inferences about the group or the topic in general in your conclusion.

Stages of Writing a Classification Essay

1. Select a topic of interest and limit it. If your instructor does not provide you with a particular topic, choose it independently and refer to the subject of your interest. For instance, you may consider the following options and use them as a basis for a classification essay:

- Evaluate local daycare options by affordability.

- Establish an individual classification criteria set for evaluating movies and TV-programs.

- Rate services (airlines, stores, online libraries) from the best to the worst.

- Use personal experience for classifying the types of modern students.

- Rate local apartments by price, age, and size.

- Classify child discipline methods and find out which of them are the best.

- Classify the electronic devices by price, quality, and ease of repair.

2. Break the topic into patterns. After your topic is selected, you should consider all the possible options of its classification and carry out some research.

3. Choose a classification principle. You need to choose the most important aspect of a certain topic and select the categories related to this aspect. Make sure that all of your categories are logically connected with each other and have the same basis of classification. For instance, if you are going to write about jobs and classify them by type of employment, you should write about freelance, part-time, and full-time jobs, but omit the details about workplace routine, difficulty, purpose, etc.

4. Consider the importance of each category. Once you have divided your topic into groups under similar classification criteria, evaluate the importance of each group and decide how you will organize your essay. You may begin with the most important group and finish by the least necessary or vice versa. The order of developing your thoughts is not as important as the inferences you will make at the end of the essay.

5. Establish the purpose of the essay. Once you have evaluated the importance of each category, set up the purpose of your writing and do your best to achieve it!

6. Put your ideas into a diagram or outline. It will help you to begin your first draft successfully, and finally organize your ideas in the most logical way.

7. Develop a thesis statement. Remember that your thesis statement should refer to the specific topic, establish a basis for categorizing, and name the groups you have developed.

8. Start writing an introduction. Open your classification essay with explaining the importance and purpose of writing, evaluate your role in the research, and explain which classification method you use and why.

9. Write topic sentences and body paragraphs. Dedicate each topic sentence to a certain element or group from your thesis statement and expand their meaning in the body paragraphs. Do not dedicate one paragraph to highlighting the specifics of two or more categories, as it will ruin the logical order of developing a thought.

10. Sum up the ideas in the conclusion. Summarize the main concepts highlighted in the body paragraphs and draw some inferences. Express the limitations of your classification, if there are any.

11. Proofread the essay. One of the biggest mistakes students make is forgetting to proofread the paper and submitting it with grammar or spelling mistakes. Proofread the paper thoroughly and correct the mistakes, if there are any.

12. Check the paper on plagiarism. Even if you did not use someone else's words, you could forget to cite all the sources properly. To avoid misunderstandings, check your paper and make sure it is 100% original.

Guidelines and Tightening Your Essay

Though the choice of the topic for a classification essay seems exceedingly difficult, there is a classical way of moving your ideas in the right direction. Look through the topics suggested below and develop your own.

1. Types of users in a social network (evaluate them by appearance, behavior, or activity).
2. Types of artists (classification by area of proficiency, popularity or artistic values).
3. Extracurricular activities (unusual, unexpected, and common).
4. The most popular ways to keep fit (diets, exercising, giving up bad habits, etc.).
5. Types of health and their importance in modern life (physical, emotional, spiritual, social, mental, and environmental).
6. Types of people commonly met in gym (classify them by reasons to come to gym, appearance or behavior models).
7. Videos people watch (consider different social media platforms (YouTube, Vimeo, Facebook), sort videos by genre, rate their viewers by age and needs.
8. Benefits in sports professions (compare football quarterbacks, soccer goalies, and baseball pitchers).
9. Evaluating the quality of customer service in a local mall (rate the stores from the worst to the best based on your personal experience).

10. Types of touristic trips (classify them by purpose: health, business, incentive, leisure, sport, special interest, etc.).

11. Computer users versus smartphone and tablet users (rate them by preferences, technical literacy, profession, etc.).

12. Accommodation alternatives for students with a limited budget (renting a flat, dormitory or staying with relatives).

13. Types of Christmas gifts and their rating by popularity (expensive presents, small but pleasant things, toys, cards).

14. Rating of the most favorable pets in different countries (compare the popularity of dogs, cats, snakes, spiders, hamsters, etc.).

15. Types of communication strategies for resolving a conflict (sort them by effectiveness, popularity, and complexity).

Mistakes to Avoid While Writing a Classification Essay

1. **Leaving a category out of attention.** If you write about healthy diet and classify the food into grains, fruits, vegetables, and protein, you cannot forget about dairy, as this group also represents an irreplaceable part of a healthy diet. In this way, make sure that you write about all essential elements of classification.

2. **Writing about too many categories.** It will blur your essay and make the classification less precise. For instance, if you write about fashion and your organizing principle is practical clothing, you wouldn't include high heels into your classification, as you would have to expand upon jeans, cotton blouses, sneakers, etc. Remember that in a classification essay you should write about the categories that are important and somehow connected with the overall purpose of the paper.

3. **Using different criteria sets.** This mistake is the most common in students' papers, as they frequently misunderstand different classification principles and try to use them all to convey a single idea. To eliminate the possibility of making this mistake, create a chart of your categories and give a name to each classification principle. Once you have done it, the logical organization of your paper is ready. Imagine that you need to write about types of sports and sort them by popularity within tourists. Writing about native water sports would not be proper, as you will expand not only on tourist benefit, but also on fitness, healthy lifestyle, fishing, etc.; additionally, you will have to classify the types of native water sports, what will ultimately destroy the logical organization of the paper.

4. **Supporting the topic with examples unequally.** Providing an unequal number of examples for some category will make a particular group less significant than others. In this way, remember that the number of examples provided for each category should be similar.

Classification Essay Writing Checklist

Introduction

- Have you determined the purpose of writing and explained in the introduction?

- Have you clearly identified the group you are categorizing?

- Have you written about your topic, categorizing principle, and groups developed in your thesis sentence?

- Does your thesis statement justify the groups chosen for deeper analysis?

Body

- Does each of your body paragraphs open with a topic sentence?

- Do your topic sentences narrow the topic of the whole paper to the topic of a particular paragraph?

- Have you maintained topic sentences by background information and descriptive details to expand readers' knowledge about a certain category?

- Is the structure of your body paragraphs and connection between them logical?

- Have you used transitions and comparisons for enhancing the structure of the main body?

- Have you blended together all the investigated categories in the concluding paragraph?

- Have you used a single classification principle?

- Haven't you forgot about any important category to write about?

- Haven't you included inappropriate or unimportant categories into your essay?

- Have you supported each category with examples equally?

- Have you established logical connections between categories?

Conclusion

- Have you made a logical inference in the conclusion (provided summary of strong and weak points of each category or emphasized the advantages of one category over the other)?

- Have you achieved the purpose of writing, established in the introductory paragraph?

Works Cited

"Division and Classification: What Are Division and Classification?" *Cengage Learning*,

infotrac.thomsonlearning.com/infowrite/ex_division.htm.

Franco, Gerald G. "Classification Essay Writing — How to Classify & Write." *Essay

Academia*,2010, essayacademia.com/classification-essay-writing-service.php.

"How to Write a Classification Essay." *AnswerShark*, https://answershark.com/writing/essay-

writing/classification-essay/how-to-write-classification-essay.html.

Nordquist, Richard. "How to Compose a Classification Essay." *About Education*, 2016. Accessed 1

Feb. 2017.

"The 40 Best Classification & Division Essay Topics to Consider." *SchoolofInteriorDesign*,

www.schoolofinteriordesign.org/classification-division-essay-topics/.

"What Is a Classification Essay?" *Essayinfo.com*. Accessed 1 Feb. 2017.

"Writing a Classification Paper." *Butte.edu*, www.butte.edu/departments/cas/tipsheets/style_

purpose_ strategy/classification.

Sample 1. Classifications for Different Types of Tourists

According to the purpose of traveling, there are diverse types of tourists: incentive, health, business, cultural, leisure, sport, and many others. Typology of tourists is an essential element of the work of travel agency managers. Before offering the client a particular program, firstly a manager should determine what type it belongs to, and then, considering the objectives and preferences, point out the best options of leisure pursuits and provide them with suitable services.

An incentive tourist is an employee who as a result of showing an excellent performance in work gets a company paid holiday as a reward. Grimaldi states that Properly designed and executed incentive travel programs can increase sales productivity by 18 percent and produce an ROI of 112 percent (15). Therefore, this accolade is in common practice within commercial firms to motivate cooperators to be more productive in further performance. Incentive tourists can participate in a golf tournament for incentive groups at the country club, ballooning, a picnic on the Alpine peaks, a cruise with music and dance evenings, drinking or gastronomic tours, etc.

Health tourists are people who are taking a trip abroad, not only to enjoy the sights but also to improve their health. A key point of such a trip is to have healthy rest opportunities amidst the favorable climate, water facilities, spa resorts, beauty of landscapes, etc. Most of the participants are deprived of the quality treatment benefits in their country, so they visit neighboring countries and the distant continents for specific types of treatment, for a diagnosis and examination or the rehabilitation and improvement of the general health state.

Business tourists' programs are restricted to the company demands, which means each participant's affiliation with conferences and meetings, exhibitions and trade fairs, corporate events, outdoor events, negotiations, market research, training and so forth. This type of tourist differs from the incentive tourist because he or she doesn't have enough time to become familiar with local cultural assets and take advantage of entertainment facilities.

Cultural tourists visit foreign countries to get a look at the history and culture of another country in all its manifestations, including architecture, painting, music, theater, folklore, traditions, customs, and the lifestyle of local people. For example, cultural tourists from Europe tend to visit prominent symbols of the United States of America (the White House, the Statue of Liberty, Mount Rushmore). Apart from this, there are frequently attended events, like the Ballooning Festival in Albuquerque, New Mexico, and the Indianapolis Motor Speedway.

According to McGuilan Leisure tourists prefer "staying in nice hotels or resorts, relaxing on beaches or in a room, or going on guided tours and experiencing local tourist attractions" (7). These tourists seek pleasure and disengage themselves from everyday affairs through experiencing extreme kinds of activities, go sunbathing and swimming, attending cruise parties, etc.

Sports tourist's target is to experience sporting event, training camp, competitions. For example, one can either participate or become a witness of sports events like European Figure Skating Championship, the Tour de France (cycling event), Sailing America's Cup, Tennis Grand Slam, etc.

The classification is important for recreation agencies to meet the expectations of their customers by identification preferable engagements. However many tourists are involved in a variety of activities during their vacation so that they can overlap into more than one category (for example, a business tourist apart from attending conferences or completing business transaction could include a tint of culture tourism into his vacation through visiting exhibitions or excursions or other activities unique to the place of sojourn.) To sum up, it should be mentioned that the classification of tourists serves as a significant tool to identify factors that stimulate people to make trips abroad.

Works Cited

Grimaldi, Lisa. "IRF Releases Top 7 Incentive Travel Statistics." *IRF Releases Top 7 Incentive Travel Statistics: Meetings & Conventions*. N.p., 17 Apr. 2015, http://www.meetings-conventions.com/News/Incentives/IRF-Releases-Top-7-Incentive-Travel-Statistics/. Accessed 26 Dec. 2016.

McGuigan, Brendan. "The Definition of a Leisure Traveler." *USA Today*. Gannett Satellite Information Network, n.d. http://traveltips.usatoday.com/definition-leisure-traveler-15302.html. Accessed 26 Dec. 2016.

Mckercher, Bob. "Towards a Classification of Cultural Tourists." *International Journal of Tourism Research* 4.1(2002). http://onlinelibrary.wiley.com/doi/10.1002/jtr.346/abstract. Accessed 28 Feb.2017.

Sample 2. First Dates

It is not a big secret that the majority of people under thirty years gain some experience in dating and can share some stories about first dates. It is clear that the number of first dates varies depending on the human temperament, the cultural environment, socialization intensity and other factors that may affect the ability and desire to go on dates. Apparently, the stories about first dates can be described by such words as funny, sad and tragic. First dates can be satisfactory or unsuccessful. In fact, the consequences and emotional response to a date are difficult to predict without going on it, so there is no need to make some predictions or create some rules. However, it is possible to classify a place for the first date by the existence of opportunities to conduct an extensive dialogue and to get a chance to know each one better.

It is clear that most people try to seek out exciting and extravagant ways to engage in a first date as much as possible, due to a formula: "First dates need two things — a chance to get to know each other and some energy" (Boyes). The most popular kind of first date is an invitation for coffee or dinner. This type of meeting offers a place for conversation. Additionally, that sort of dating can inform about the ability to communicate with the staff, to respond to the possible unpleasant situations from the environment, and the tastes in food. Another advantage of this type of dating is that it can be easily transform into another kind of activity, which may be a walk in the park or near the lake. Such activities also offer many opportunities for conversation. Naturally, one can start the first date with a walk, and then finish with a dinner.

A popular activity on the first date is a trip to museums, a zoo or a botanical garden.(Fuller) This type of dating helps the couple to conduct an active dialogue, as the environment's subjects bring some topics for conversation, and expel the fear of awkward silence that may arise between people on the first date. Another popular place for the first date is a date at the movie theater, but this type of dating can not provide the real dialogue between the pair, and therefore will not help them get acquainted. Also, watching the film in the dark may bring about the unusual situation where nobody knows whether to take the mate's hand or put the head on the partner's shoulder. Of course, if a movie is combined with dinner or a walk, the possibility increases for a good first date.

Another popular type of first date is engaging in an activity (skating, sailing, water sports, kayaking) (Rimonte). This kind of dating is the worst for people who primarily want to meet and know each other because all physical activities require focus on the movements and safety rules. Besides, a person may worry about how cleverly and beautifully they perform physical actions.

Since the success of the first date depends on many factors, it is no use to calculate carefully every detail. The most important in the first date is personal intentions and plans for future development of the relationship. However, it is important to remember that not every popular place for the first date can offer a chance to have a deep conversation.

Works Cited

Boyes, Alice. "21 First Date Ideas." *Psychology Today*, 2013, https://www.psychologytoday.com /blog/in-practice/201312/21-first-date-ideas.

Fuller, Tara. "29 Awesome First Date Ideas That Don't Involve Sitting at a Bar." *Greatist*, 2015, http://greatist.com/play/first-date-ideas.

Rimonte, Roxanne. *"8 Types of First Dates Every Girl Will Go Through."* *Thought Catalog*, 2015, http://thoughtcatalog.com/roxanne-rimonte/2015/07/8-types-of-first-dates-every-girl-will-go-through/.

Chapter 4. Evaluation Essay Writing Guide

Imagine yourself discussing your favorite movie with your friends and proving that the film of your choice is the most appropriate option to watch. How are you going to stand up for your opinion? Undoubtedly, you'll have to provide a comprehensive review of this movie, use examples and judgment to prove that it is worth watching. The same you will be doing when working on your evaluation essay, which is why writing it wouldn't be a problem for you!

What's So Special About Evaluation Essay Writing?

An evaluation essay is like a review: your main purpose is to judge whether a concept is bad or good in comparison with the other. A good evaluation essay does not only indicate the idea but stands on the ground of its author, proving WHY something is good or bad. To write an effective evaluation essay, you will need to establish a criteria set for evaluation, and provide solid evidence and representative examples to help readers form an opinion about the subject of your writing.

You are familiar with evaluation essays if you've read numerous reviews on the books, movies or products of your interest. An evaluation essay can be different in tone: feel free to be funny, sarcastic, official or earnest, as your main purpose is to provide a persuasive and effective review of the topic, idea, or product. In this way, remember that using evidence, judgment, and a specific criteria is critical for effective presentation of your opinion. Without these integral elements, the evaluation essay is unlikely to be persuasive enough.

Evaluation Essay Structure

Though the structure of all academic papers is relatively similar, the content is significantly different. Let's explore how to make the content of your evaluation paper convenient to the norms and rules of academic writing.

1. Introduction. The introductory paragraph of an evaluation essay should refer to the subject or idea being evaluated and provide supplementary information about it. For instance, if the student writes an evaluation paper about a book, he or she may refer to the writing style of the author, critical evaluation, popularity, previous editions, and plot of the book. In this way, the main purpose of the introductory paragraph is to introduce the topic to your readers.

2. Thesis statement. The thesis statement is typically put into the last one or two sentences of the introductory paragraph. The thesis should reflect the main idea of the essay and provide criteria for evaluation. For instance, if you write about the book and evaluate its plot, you may write about positive role models, good characters, or unexpectable narrative moves, because these elements all together make the storyline of each book amazing.

3. Main body: topic sentences. To make the structure of your essay clear, it is essential to organize your thoughts and develop arguments in a logical order. You should start each body paragraph with a topic sentence that will put the reader in a topic and serve as a logical beginning of an idea. A topic sentence, just like a body paragraph, should be dedicated to a single

idea, not a combination of the ideas. For instance, if you write about the plot of the book, your topic sentence should highlight only one component of the plot (unexpectable events, positive behavior models or good characters). Mixing all the components up will make the structure of the paper complicated and inconsequent.

4. Main body: body paragraphs. After writing an informative topic sentence, you should expand the focus of the sentence, supplement it by the results of the judgment and add supporting evidence to your body paragraph. In other words, each body paragraph should highlight one criterion out of the criteria set mentioned in the thesis. For instance, if your topic sentence is about unexpectable events as the key component of the plot, your body paragraph should list the specific events which make this plot effective. Organizing your thoughts in such manner will make the evaluation essay easier for comprehension and more persuasive, so do not mix up your ideas and work on a proper structure for the paper.

5. Conclusion. Typically, the concluding paragraph of an evaluation essay provides a final comment based on the criteria set from the thesis. The author should ultimately decide whether the evaluated subject is worth using or not, indicate the groups of people who are the most likely to use this product, and express limitations to the topic if there are any.

Stages of Writing an Evaluation Essay

A good evaluation essay requires preparing a thorough analysis, developing a strong opinion, and judging and evaluating the subject with the help of established criteria. Though an evaluation essay encourages injecting some opinion, it should not be opinionated! A good evaluation essay is aimed at discussing the quality of the product or service, remaining unbiased and reasoned. To go through all of these steps successfully, follow the suggested below stages for evaluation essay writing.

1. Brainstorm subjects to write about. Choose a topic that is close to your experiences, interests, and values. It will help you to establish evaluation criteria and develop an opinion about the topic. In an evaluation essay, it is essential to concentrate on a particular business, service, policy, or product. That is to say that you should focus on the specific class, but not on a group of classes, so narrow your topic down to its integral elements and write about them. The following list of classes and their elements will help you to find a convenient topic:

Performances: play, concert, movie, fashion show, sporting event, advertising campaign

Experiences: store, restaurant, club, event, vacation, studying program

Products: website, album, book, technological device, clothing brand, luxury item

Places: park, museum, zoo, unique building, concert venue, sports stadium

2. Establish criteria for evaluation. Finding criteria means establishing the ideal of the product or service. Criteria are integral parts of a product's quality that allow you to judge something as good or bad. For instance, when evaluating the listed above categories, you may use the following criteria set or establish your own:

Movie: plot, scenery, cast, directing, score, humor, actors' professionalism, etc.

Book: content, writing style, ease of navigation, design, plot, author's individual style, etc.

Restaurant: atmosphere, service quality, food, price, value, and taste

3. Judge the subject. Judgment is the detection of places where the criterion is not met. In other words, judgment requires establishing connections between evaluating criteria and the subject of your interest. Using the judgment helps to formulate an opinion about the subject. For instance, if the analyzed restaurant does not provide high-quality service and food, it cannot be called a good place to stay in.

4. Look for supporting evidence. Support your judgment with relevant facts, materials, and the results of your own investigation. It will back up your opinion and make your position stronger. For instance, if you indicate that the analyzed restaurant does not provide a high-quality service,

you will need to find and use many representative examples to show how this judgment was formed.

5. Transform it all into an essay. Write down the most important ideas found in the result of your evaluation. Indicate your topic, the established criteria, the opinion you defend, and elements of supplementary evidence. It will systematize your thinking and establish a basis for a good evaluation essay.

6. Create an informative introduction. In an evaluation essay, the introduction paragraph should grab readers' attention and provide background to the topic. For instance, if you evaluate the restaurant, you may dedicate the introduction to its history, founders, customer satisfaction rates, and overall popularity of the place.

7. Come up with an effective thesis sentence. The thesis statement should reflect the idea of the whole essay, which is why you should present your opinion in a clear, persuasive, and unbiased manner. It is highly recommended to put the thesis statement in the last sentence of the introductory paragraph. A powerful thesis sentence should present the opinion and list several arguments to support it. Example: *McDonald's has the reputation of a high-quality time-saving fast food restaurant: prices are respective to value, the atmosphere is fun and friendly, food is tasty and original, and the quality of the service is consistently high.*

8. Develop supporting arguments in the main body. Start each body paragraph with a topic sentence that should put the reader into the picture of the paragraph's main idea. An example of the topic sentence: *McDonald's does not offer the lowest price, but it provides a high value for its price spectrum.* Further, you should extend the focus of the topic sentence and develop the idea in the body paragraph with the help of supporting evidence. For instance, when writing about the value and prices range in McDonald's, you should discuss high-quality ingredients, nutritional characteristics of the food, special offers, and economic opportunities.

9. Sum it all up in a conclusion. Restate your thesis statement once again and make your readers feel that they have visited the restaurant with you. Encourage them to agree with the results of your evaluation and briefly summarize the main ideas highlighted in the body paragraphs.

10. Proofread and edit the paper. Focus on the tone, writing style, order of developing arguments, overall persuasiveness and reliability of the paper. Identify potential grammatical and spelling mistakes and correct them. Check your paper for plagiarism and omit any accusations of academic misconduct.

Guidelines and Tightening Your Essay

Though instructions for writing an evaluation essay are clear and easy-to-follow, your essay should not look like a naked outline of the facts and arguments. Instead, your essay should be extraordinary, reflect your individual writing style, provide a comprehensive evaluation of the topic, and encourage the readers to believe in your words. Here are several tips that will help you to make your evaluation essay original and unique.

Extraordinary presentation of the subject. Undoubtedly, almost a half of the essay's success depends on the appropriate presentation of the subject. Due to this, you should provide readers with a range of details, including all the information you need to explain to the reader what you initially wanted to. Besides this, you should do your best to help readers take on your position, so do not use controversial details — they will make a review more complicated, and the readers will be less likely to agree with your opinion.

Objective evaluation equals a quality review. Remember that you are writing an evaluation essay, so do not transform it into a summary. The analytical part of your paper with evidence, judgment, and criteria should be no less than two-thirds of the paper. Accordingly, the summary of the topic being evaluated should be no more than one-third of the essay. Besides this, make sure that your evaluation is accurate and clear, as defending biased opinions or taking on unreasoned positions is strictly forbidden in this type of academic writing. Focus on the quality of the product, service or item you are analyzing, switch on "the objectiveness mode" and prepare an irresistible evaluation essay.

Make the judgment authoritative and clear. First, it is essential to write what you think; otherwise, it will be difficult for you to stay objective. Second, you should identify your target audience and make the paper appropriate to its needs. Third, you should take notes on the topic being investigated. Divide your notes into three columns (criteria, judgment, evidence) and use this information in the essay. Remember that you should use at least three criteria to make evaluation comprehensive.

Stay passionate but concrete. Remember what we said about the tone of the paper? Feel free to experiment with different tones but stay objective. For instance, you may write in a passionate manner, demonstrating the audience how immersed in the topic you are. Nevertheless, do not forget to use supporting evidence to back up your arguments and order your paragraphs in a logical manner (from the least to the most important).

Defend your judgment. Do not forget about the power of quotations, anecdotes, thoughts of experts, contrasts and comparisons. These little details are essential for the overall effectiveness of the paper.

Use secret instruments. In this type of academic paper, you can experiment with a wide range of tricks, and here are some of the most impressive.

1. Contrast & compare. Compare the analyzed subject with the best equivalent in the same genre. For instance, you may take an unpopular political doctrine and compare it with political views of your favorite president. You can identify the group the evaluated subject belongs to (literary genre, clothing style, etc.) and contrast individual characteristics of the subject with features of the group.

2. Unfulfilled expectations. This tip is especially effective in this type of academic writing. Open your paper and describe what you were expecting to see before evaluating the subject, then express whether the subject is worse or better than you anticipated.

3. Diversified analysis. You may analyze the topic not only by criteria but by chronological order, social context, overall importance, influence, etc. You may evaluate any subject that you like, starting from visual art and finishing by clothing brand.

Evaluation Essay Topic Ideas

To help you master the art of diversified analysis, here are examples of topics that will inspire you!

1. Weather forecast programs and their predictions (accuracy, popularity, competency).

2. Comparing home-cooked meals with fast food (nutritional value, taste, affordability, convenience).

3. Evaluating several mobile phone apps with the same purpose (design, price, interface, effectiveness, popularity).

4. Comparing the textbook and educational software (efficiency, popularity, affordability, up-to-dateness).

5. Evaluating golf as a unique kind of sport (importance, influence of stars, popularity on television, difference from other types of sports).

6. Comparing recent and classical romance movies (roles of men and women, critical evaluation, popularity on the television, contemporaneity, professionalism of actors, plot differences).

7. Evaluating the profession of a teacher/ lawyer/ doctor (wage, professional duties, routine, satisfaction rates, qualification, studying process, retirement age).

8. Comparing laptop and desktop computer user experience (price range, design, functionality, flexibility, technical abilities).

9. Evaluating the factors which make advertising effective (consumerism era, human factor, marketing pressure).

10. Comparing the experience of playing a computer sports-related game and participating in sports competition (emotional condition, physical activeness, brain work, health impact).

11. Playing different roles by the same actress/ actor (adopting different roles, criticism and awards, meeting director's demands).

12. Comparing a Mexican and Italian restaurant (dining experience, quality of service, taste, and flavors).

13. Evaluating the supermarket as an alternative to fast food service (price, health impact, ingredients, convenience).

14. Comparing several technology opportunities that help in education (PowerPoint presentations, educational blogs, video clips, posts on Facebook and Twitter).

15. Evaluating swimming as an individual sport (commitment, practice, difficulty, health benefits and risks, difference from team sport).

Mistakes to Avoid While Writing an Evaluation Essay

Though an evaluation essay is almost similar to a review, it has a set of specific demands that should necessarily be followed by any student. Here is the list of the most common mistakes to help you transform your piece of writing into a real masterpiece.

1. **Summarizing too much.** This is the golden rule of each effective evaluation essay, as writing a review has nothing in common with detailed summarizing. The majority of students face difficulties when having to explain their own thoughts, so they summarize a lot, forgetting about the main purpose of each evaluation essay. In this way, you

should not summarize the plot when evaluating your favorite book, but identify which factors make this plot attractive, explain why this book is a must to read, and evaluate the mastery and individual style of the author. Of course, you should provide some background on the topic you write about, so put a brief overview (about three sentences) into the introduction. Do not forget that the main purpose of the evaluation essay is not to tell what the idea (product, service) is about, but to investigate and explain why this idea is good or bad.

2. **Making your writing trivial.** Students like using cliches, don't they? These words and phrases are so sweet-sounding and attractive, that it becomes impossible to avoid them. However, overwhelming an evaluation essay with cliches is entirely inappropriate, as it will make your thoughts less valuable and objective. Due to this, try explaining all the thoughts in your own words, do not use those classic phrases which make your ideas unreasonable and meaningless. Additionally, you should avoid overstatements, as they have no scientific value and seem to be biased. To help you on the pathway to a proper word choice, here are some of the words and phrases strongly recommended to avoid: "a must-see," "the best idea of the year," "a feel-good product," "a masterpiece," "a classic hit," "an inspiring artwork," etc.

3. **Using colloquial language.** Some students misunderstand the requirements of academic style, as they write in the same manner of how they communicate in a day-to-day routine. However, an evaluation essay is a type of academic writing, so it should be built and structured according to the demands of a formal style. Due to this, you should write in an official manner, use an objective tone, operate strong facts, and write in an academic language. In this way, using first-person and second-person pronouns, emotional expressions, and slang words is strictly forbidden in students' papers. Avoiding these elements will facilitate your academic success and bring significantly beneficial results.

Evaluation Essay Writing Checklist

As soon as your essay is finished, go through this checklist and evaluate your results independently:

Introduction

- Have you provided a brief overview (about three sentences) of the evaluated subject in the introduction?

- Have you included thesis statement into the last sentence of the introductory paragraph? Does it reflect the main idea of the essay and provide criteria for evaluation? Does your thesis present an opinion and several arguments to support it?

- Is the topic of the evaluation paper introduced comprehensively in the introduction?

Body

- Have you started each body paragraph from a topic sentence?

- Is each topic sentence dedicated to a single idea that is further developed in the body paragraph?

- Have you arranged the ideas highlighted in the body paragraphs logically? Did you start from the least and finish by the most important?

- Does your essay contain judgment, evaluation criteria, and evidence to support your arguments?

- Have you supported your judgment by quotations, anecdotes, thoughts of experts, contrasts or comparisons?

- Is the tone of your essay objective and unbiased?

- Have you used at least one "secret instrument" (unfulfilled expectations, comparison and contrast, diversified analysis)?

- Have you presented and evaluated your subject in an extraordinary manner?

Conclusion

- Have you summarized all of the arguments in the conclusion?

- Have you encouraged the readers to adopt your point of view in the conclusion?

- Does your paper avoid looking like a summary of the subject you investigate?

- Did you achieve the purpose of your writing? Do the results of the evaluation satisfy your expectations?

Works Cited

"How to Write an Evaluation Essay." *AcademicHelp,* www.academichelp.net, 2012. Accessed 21 Feb. 2017.

"How to Write a Critical Evaluation Essay." *Anoka-Ramsey,* www.anokaramsey.edu. Accessed 21 Feb.2017.

Kearney, Virginia. "How to Write an Evaluation Paper With Sample Essays." *LetterPile,* 2016. Accessed 21 Feb. 2017.

Kearney, Virginia. "100 Evaluation Essay Topic Ideas." *LetterPile,* 2016. Accessed 21 Feb. 2017.

Roach, Kelly. "Evaluative Essay: Examples, Format & Characteristics." *Study.com.* 2017. Accessed 21 Feb. 2017.

"The Evaluation Essay." *Aims.edu,* 2016. Accessed 21 Feb. 2017.

Sample 1. Does a Sport Teach to Compete, or to Work in a Team?

Going in for sports teaches people many things, helps to maintain discipline and makes people healthy. Sport develops initiative, allowing person overcome difficulties. And of course, being a sportsman means being competitive and being involved in the particular sphere within a certain group of individuals of same goals and interests. It is impossible to state that a sport teaches either competing or working in a team, as it contributes to both of these abilities.

Firstly, playing team games contributes significantly to such professional skills as working in the team, cooperation, sharing and to distributing responsibilities. Being involved in sports activities presupposes being responsible both for personal performance, and for the success of the team. Also, athletes develop such qualities as the ability to provide with a helping hand and give a piece of advice, as well as to be sympathetic and humane. According to Bob Stewart and Sarah Powell, those who are involved in some kind of sports activities since childhood learn very quickly how to communicate with people (35-38). Going in for sports also means communication with people. When children are brought up in certain society with peers who have mutual interests and goals, it is easier for them to commune with others during adulthood. Also, those who are in for sports learn to be faithful, honest, brave and patient. One who is sportive is not shy, and is initiative instead. All these qualities help people to work in team with people, to cooperate successfully and to feel oneself firmly and confidently among peers.

Secondly, being a sportsman develops the correct attitude towards competition in any other sphere of life. At the very beginning of the sports career, no matter what kind of sport is considered, people are put into the competitive environment. To this competitive environment belong other sportsmen, if it is a single kind of sports or opponent teams. The proper attitude towards competition, in fact, is frequently underestimated and considered as something negative. To compete is not wishing failure to the opposite side as many may think. It is realizing personal advantages, as well as being aware of different approaches to the things within a sphere. A competition is a sort of non-verbal communication, and an assessment of our skills, standards and level in comparison with others (Smith, Jay K.). Those who have at least once found themselves in such an environment learn how to win honorably and to lose with dignity. Such people have an adequate attitude towards critics, they are not afraid of changes as they want to stay competitive. Competition teaches us many things: not to be afraid to lose, to be confident while performing, and to be responsible for success.

Competition and ability to work in the team are tightly connected, as working in the team sometimes means competition within a team, or outside of it. Each team leader should at least once feel himself or herself in a competitive environment to realize either power or weak points of the own team. And each team member should also be engaged in competition, to be motivated to try best for the sake of the team. Being abreast of vicarious results motivate teams to be more cooperative and united. That is why I am deeply convinced that a sport teaches both to compete and to work in a team and that these two issues are tightly connected and add to each other.

Works Cited

Smith, Jay K. "How to Achieve Team Cohesion Through Competition in Sport: An Organizational Model." *The Sport Journal*, 2015, United States Sports Academy, http://thesportjournal.org/article/how-to-achieve-team-cohesion-through-competition-in-sport-an-organizational-model/.Accessed 10 Mar. 2017.

Stewart, Bob and Sarah Powell. "Team Building and Team Working." *Team Performance Management: An International Journal*, vol 10, no. 1/2, 2004, pp. 35-38. Emerald.

Sample 2. The Rules and Structure of the Playoff System for a Sport

A playoff system in sports competitions is a system of organization, in which the participant is eliminated from the tournament after the first loss from a single game or series of several games between the two opponents. This approach allows for the identification of the unconditional winner. It provides the identification of the winner with the minimum number of stages and promotes a tense competition in the tournament. This is a perfect way of distributing places when there is a large number of teams.

Principles of pairs selection on the first stage may be different: casting lots is mostly used, although selection according to the rating is possible. According to Vorob'ev, the advantages of the playoffs include the minimum number of games comparing with other options of tournaments, as well as being uncompromising — it is neither possible nor sensible to contract draws (1994). Play-offs are aimed to identify strengths and to provide a fair understanding who deserves the first place as fast as possible. According to Laan Herings and Talman, the playoff system is not suitable for tournaments, where it is important to ensure an equitable distribution of all places, not only from the first to the third (2000). In the playoffs, all places except the first ones are first distributed, and at the end of the tournament, the first, second and third are distributed. To exclude the possibility of meetings of the strongest participants in the first round and to raise interest in sports games, the last series of the competition sometimes has a so-called "dispersion" of the most influential participants.

As it has already been mentioned, the system can only identify a winner who deserves the first place. In cases where it is necessary or desirable to determine and place the rest of the participants, additional games are conducted. The member who was eliminated from the competition in the final gets second place and the losers in the semi-finals play the extra game, and the winner gets third place, and the loser — fourth one.

The selection of pairs very strongly influences the results. "In the case of the draw, the last places are distributed almost randomly: a weak party can easily rise above the strong, who got an even stronger opposite in the first round (Herings, Laan, & Talman, 2000)." The rules keep teams in constant competition between each other, as inevitably one participant from the pair leaves the game.

Playoffs are widely used in national and international competitions in team sports. Another name for the playoff structure is "Olympic system." It is due to the fact that this order is essential for team sports at the Olympics.

This system is perfect for such tournaments which have a significant number of teams. It is almost impossible to identify the winner among teams in another way. It keeps the participants motivated, as this competition does not give a team or a single player any right on a mistake. But for a tournament which has a small amount of teams, it is not reliable to imply payoff method, as last places may be distributed incorrectly.

Works Cited

Herings, P., Laan, G., & Talman, D. *Cooperative Games in Graph Structure* (1st ed.), 2000.

Vorob'ev, N. *Foundations of Game Theory* (1st ed.), 1994. Basel: Birkhäuser Basel.

Chapter 5. Reflective Essay Writing Guide

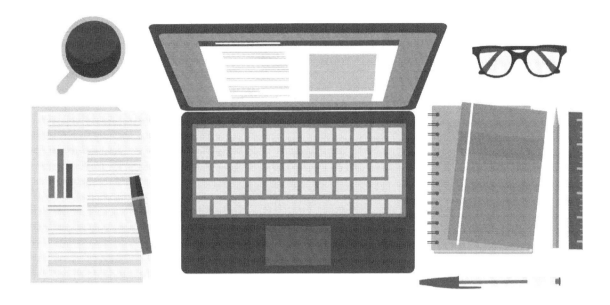

That's it. You are holding in your arms a piece of paper that gives you some strange news: you have to write a reflective essay.

Keep calm. A reflective essay is just a paper about you and your thoughts. That's why you should concentrate and take a couple of breaths — in and out.

This essay should come from inside of you, as it reveals your own thoughts which may be lying inside your mind. Discover yourself from the deep – it's a very important part of you.

What's So Special about a Reflective Essay?

Perhaps, you have already written several types of essays during your classes but you just can't get how reflective essays differ from others. So, what is a reflective essay?

A reflective essay is a type of academic paper that reflects your personality, and describes the scene of events that influenced your knowledge and experience. For example, a student from a medical university comes to practice in a real hospital and describes what problems he or she faced and how they were solved, what new experiences were gained, and what his or her hopes and expectations were before practicing and if they were fulfilled.

Generally speaking, reflective writing differs from academic, as it focuses on your own experience. In reflective writing you don't need to use literature — the entire paper is build upon your own experience. Also, you should express your own view instead of comparing the views of others. And the final distinctive thing is writing the paper from the first person perspective and the frequent use of "I" statements (whereas academic writing forbids the use of "I" in sentences).

While a good reflective essay shows the reader a clear idea of how some experience influenced your life, thoughts and emotions, you should also be creative enough to present your thoughts in a clear and interesting manner.

Types of Reflective Essays

This type of essay is usually assigned to students in order to check how they mastered the program and how they will adapt to a professional experience. Assignments may be of such types:

1. Reflective essay on literature: this assignment requires from the student not only to read a book or piece of writing, but also to understand it, reflect upon its content and compare with his or her own personal experience.

2. Reflective essay in the professional sphere: students that are on practice (social workers, doctors and teachers) are assigned to write reflective essays in order to see how they behave with other people from the other side and understand how they can improve their knowledge or attitude.

3. Reflective essay in education. Teachers may give you such an assignment after a lecture in order to help you and your classmates understand the material better.

4. Reflective essay for personal growth. If you attend writing classes, you will be frequently assigned such essays as they help you understand yourself, analyze personal experiences and become more confident.

Contrary to other essay types, reflective essays don't require in-depth research on a certain topic or any calculations. The nature of such essays is very personal and depends on your reflection only on a certain event, so it has no strict structure and style. But hold on! Before you start writing your reflective essay, please, read the instructions.

Reflective Essay Writing Structure

While subjects of your future essays may vary from one to another, the structure will remain the same. You will definitely begin your essay with an introduction, describe the main parts in the body and end with a conclusion. Reflective essays have some distinctive features that we will cover in the following sections.

Introduction

Every essay needs an introduction and your reflective essay is not an exception. The introduction is divided into several sections and traditionally they are:

• Attention grabber (or hook) that will concentrate the reader's attention on your paper from the very beginning. If your paper will be about your experience, you can start with a prompt preview of the most interesting moments from your story.

• A thesis statement that reveals the heart of your story. For a reflective essay, it may be a description of a person or event that greatly influenced you and served a purpose to this essay. Please, remain short in words, as the following paragraph will totally expand further on these facts.

Body

This part of the essay outline may be considered as the most important. As every reflective essay is by nature unique, we can't give you detailed steps of writing it. But in order to organize your thoughts in a good reflective essay and to avoid missing the information, you can pay attention to the following tips:

- Don't forget about chronology. Make the list of events in chronological order as they appeared in your life and mark them appropriately. You are not required to write strictly about every life episode with the dates, just keep in mind that it will be hard for the reader to delve into the essence of your story if facts frequently jump from one time to another.

- Make sure that your reflective essay should strictly describe the impact of the particular place, event or person on your experience and knowledge. This part is usually the most interesting for readers, so try to present it fascinatingly and add as much detail as possible.

For example, if you need to write a reflective essay about *The Little Prince*, the outline may look like this:

    I. When I first heard the story of *The Little Prince*.

        A. Description of how it happened.

        B. I have understood that the book is much more interesting than the play and this book is not just a story.

    II. How I see the plot.

        A. Description of the story.

        B. I've understood how differently grown-ups and children see life and it's a cruel reality.

    III. How I see symbolism in the story.

        A. Description of symbols in text.

IV. My favorite part of the story — meeting the fox.

    A. Description of this part.

    B. I've understood how important it is to show love to our closest ones and these little things are very important in our lives.

V. How I understood the book.

    A. I've deeply understood human nature and how many kinds of people live on earth.

    B. Everyone is looking for their own happiness and to live peacefully — just know that there are foxes (friends) and snakes (ill-wishers) around you.

    C. We must cherish our own lives, as we only get to experience them once.

We recommend you to use the following suggestions for phrases that you can use in your reflective essay:

1. For me, the most important/ meaningful/useful/significant…

2. I have enriched/developed/upgraded/improved…

3. Having experienced/ discussed/ learned/ applied…

4. This knowledge will be/ is useful/important…

5. Alternatively, this is perhaps/ might be…

6. Initially/ Previously/ Later, I felt/noticed/ realized/ thought…

7. Because I have not yet/ do not yet know/understand…

Conclusion

The finishing touch of your masterpiece will be the conclusion. It gathers all main points of your story in a brief summary (including a personal reflection on this story). But don't simply rewrite what you have already written in the introduction — avoid repetitions.

The following tips and questions will help you write a conclusion for your reflective essay more properly:

1. Draw conclusions to this situation and justify them.

2. Think about how you will act if such situation will repeat. Will you act in the same way or somehow different?

3. Has this experience influenced your own understanding of the subject or discipline?

4. Think about new questions that may arise as a result of this experience.

5. Did you discover something new about yourself?

6. Will this experience be useful in your future professional life?

Steps of Writing a Reflective Essay

No matter how skillful you are at essay writing, a good plan will help you find motivation and inspiration, and it will save your time. Discover your best working conditions and read these steps.

Step 1. Read the assignment. Your teacher may assign you a certain topic that you should write about or a certain type of experience. Read it attentively and ask your tutor questions if you can't understand something.

Step 2. Create a timetable. Planning is an essential part of every project, so take a blank paper and write down the deadline on it. Look through your timetable, classes and possible homework and, as an example, assign an hour per day for writing your essay. Also, it will be a good idea to have a pen and paper in your bag so that you can write at any moment.

Step 3. Gather the data and brainstorm. For a reflective essay this means that you will think more about people and events that brought you some experience, emotions or new knowledge. Mark the most interesting and fascinating points.

Step 4. Create the first draft. You can begin at any paragraph you want. Some students may experience writer's block when thinking about the introduction, so it will be wise to put it at the end of the writing.

Step 5. Revise the first draft. Here you should look through your text and assess its readability, sense and tone of voice. Print your text on paper and make marks near sentences that need correction or additional information.

Step 6. Check and polish. Print your final version on paper and check it for grammar errors, misspellings and other mistakes. Polish your text with transition phrases and words to make the text smoother and more readable. And don't forget about the logical structure – your text should be easily understood by the audience.

If you find it hard to write your reflective essay, don't be upset! Maybe you just need more time to think about your paper, so be sure that you dedicate enough time and effort for your writing. Set the right priorities and plan your time wisely and you will reach this goal.

Guidelines and Tightening Your Essay

Another important thing in essay writing is choosing a topic. Success of your future reflective essay totally depends on a good topic, but many students underestimate it.

How to Find a Good Topic for a Reflective Essay

1. Find a topic that is closely connected with you and your experience. A reflective essay usually focuses on a certain episode in your life, and it will be easier to write about it than turning on your imagination and creating a nonexistent situation. So, if you have never been to a summer camp, don't choose it as the basis for your topic. This advice may sound obvious, but many students frequently fail because of such a mistake.

2. Choose a topic that excites you the most. You will be surprised how writing be joyful and easy if you write about something interesting for you. You may have experienced many different situations in your life that could be described in your reflective essay, but if you

feel bored about some topics, just imagine how bored your readers will be while reading your paper. Good reflective essays effect bright emotions, so try to make your paper more engaging and exciting!

3. Pick a reflective essay topic that you can present at an unusual point of view. This skill you will need while writing a future admission essay for a college or university. Your readers (and selection committee) don't want to read a standard answer to common questions that have already been written for thousands of times. A unique approach to a common situation will make for a more interesting paper to write and read.

Good Reflective Essay Topics

Personal topics about the writer are very popular among students, as it sounds easy to write about yourself. Also, such topics can help you to find answers to some problems and serve as a free psychotherapy.

1. What personal qualities make me strong in this world and how do they help me every day?
2. What personal qualities bother me during everyday life? How can I change them?
3. How have I beaten my greatest fear?
4. Describe the most outstanding accomplishment you have ever done.
5. Tell about your first love and how you understood that those feelings were love.
6. Describe a situation when you wanted something that wasn't yours.
7. Tell about your best weekend ever.
8. What was the most memorable holiday in your life?
9. Tell about your first date and all the feelings that you experienced that time.
10. What person inspires you the most? What qualities do you appreciate?
11. Describe your ideal partner for life and what qualities he or she should have.
12. Tell about your relationship with a family member.

13. Describe how you have gained new skills (painting, cycling, hiking, swimming, etc.)

14. Tell about the best present that you have ever received.

15. Describe a situation when you were robbed or you became a victim of an accident.

Questions to Develop a Reflective Essay

It is much easier to construct your reflective essay by answering the following questions. Consider that any answer may serve as your thesis statement and help you escape from writer's block.

- What feelings did I experience?

- What moments caused those feelings? Why?

- How have those feelings influence my experience? How did I come to understand this?

- What could I have done differently?

- Have I ever experienced a similar situation to this one? How does the current experience differ from the previous one?

- Have I changed with the help of this experience? In what way?

- What can I learn from this experience?

- Did my point of view change after this experience?

- What questions should I ask myself?

- How can this experience be applied to my everyday life?

Mistakes to Avoid While Reflective Essay Writing

While many students are sure that a reflective essay is just a piece of cake, many of them still make many mistakes like the following:

1. **Writing an essay without a thesis statement.** Be sure that you have written several sentences that summarize your experience and a little description of the situation that led to this experience. You can write it after completing the body paragraph and include it into your introduction.

2. **Trying to reveal several experiences in one essay.** A reflective essay should describe a single experience that has given the most valuable lesson.

3. **Skipping the use of academic language.** Even though reflective essays are less academic than argumentative essays, your tone and words should remain academic. It is acceptable to use the "I" statement in your reflective writing, but don't overuse it.

4. **Presenting not enough information.** Be sure that you have described enough information so that readers can understand how you got that experience.

5. **Bad structure.** If your text is incoherent and it's hard to see the line of ideas that you are trying to express in your paper, readers will be confused.

6. **Forgetting to write about emotions and your own point of view.** Remember that reflective essays should describe not only the situation, but also your emotions, thoughts and conclusions about the experience you have had.

7. **Using plague words and phrases.**

8. **Writing the essay like a personal diary**, forgetting that this paper is for the writing course.

Reflective Essay Writing Checklist

Introduction

- Have you written in two or three sentences some information about what kind of experience are you going to tell the reader?

- Is your topic stated clearly?

- Have you used an attention grabber?

- Consider the fact that your introduction should increase the reader's interest in your paper.

Body

- Does the paragraph reveal enough facts and reasoning to cover your topic?

- Have you added enough details to support your thoughts and feelings?

- Have you used the right chronology of facts? Does it confuse the reader?

- Have you included moral, ethical, social or historical context into your reflective writing if it's relevant?

- Have you taken a look at your experience from another point? Maybe you could have solved the situation in another way?

- Make sure that you don't overwhelm your paper with too many details. Stay concise and to the point.

- Keep in mind the fact that you are describing your experience.

Conclusion

- Make sure that you have summarized the main points of your paper.

- Does your conclusion repeat the plot of your essay in a brief form?

- Does it leave an impression about your paper?

- Imagine that someone else is reading your paper: what emotions will he or she experience?

Works Cited

Page, Mary, and Carrie Winstanley. "Writing Essays for Dummies." Chichester: Wiley, 2009.

"Essay Writing — The Easy Way." The English Department at Colegio Anglo Colombiano. 2008. https://ontheroad29.wikispaces.com/file/view/How to Write an Essay.pdf. Accessed 15 Dec. 2016.

Kearney, Virginia. "How to Write a Reflective Essay with Sample Essays." *LetterPile,* 2016. https://letterpile.com/writing/How-to-Write-a-Reflective-Essay-with-Sample-Essays/. Accessed 15 Dec. 2016.

Meirow, E. "Use This Reflective Essay Outline to Get Your Paper Started." *Kibin Blog,* 2015. https://www.kibin.com/essay-writing-blog/reflective-essay-outline/. Accessed 13 Dec. 2016.

Hampton, M. "Reflective Writing: A Basic Introduction." 2010. http://www.port.ac.uk/media/ contacts-and-departments/student-support-services/ask/downloads/Reflective-writing-a-basic-introduction.pdf. Accessed 15 Dec.2016.

"Reflective Writing." James Cook University Australia. https://www.jcu.edu.au/__data/assets/pdf_file/0004/202666/How-to-write-a-reflective-essay.pdf. Accessed 13 Dec. 2016.

Sample 1. Looking at the Full Moon from the Roof of Your House

I think that the moon is not just Earth's satellite. Exactly the same as the sun, the moon has left a huge mark on human culture since the beginning of time. Perhaps this is because they are watching us all the time and light the way we go, whether it is day or night. The moon to some extent is the opposite of the sun. Since the sun shines during the day, it is associated with bustling activity in the streets, people rushing back and forth, the noise of the roads and an uncountable number of diverse sounds. On the contrary, the moon reflects the silence of the night. While the sun is a huge ball of fire with incredibly powerful energy raging inside, the moon embodies coldness and endless tranquility. It attracts me with its mystery and silence. Looking at it, you involuntarily plunge into the whirl of thoughts about human origins, our place in the universe, and whether there is life on the other side of that silver disk. "It is the only celestial a body beyond Earth that has been visited by human beings" (Dunbar "The Moon").

Watching the moon is my hobby. I learned this from my grandfather. When I was a child, every night he sat me on his knee and told about space, stars, constellations, black holes, quarks, the milky way, and many other "cosmic things." At the time, I was surprised that he was not talking about an object that attracts the eye the most. While he, waving his hand, had explained to me the difference between the Big Dipper and the small one, I looked at the moon trying to see something that is not visible to the human eye.

Now, I often get out onto the roof, lay down on the cold slate, and fix my eyes on the distant white lantern in the sky. Surprisingly, when I look at the moon, my thoughts whirl in my head as if in the background, like I am just a spectator not participating in my own thinking. Thoughts, in fact, are almost always the same. In such moments, I usually attempt to find answers to questions that no one knows the answers. How we appeared, how will we disappear, why we live, what is my purpose and whether that purpose exists or is it just fiction. This kind of philosophy has no end, and probably should not have. Sometimes, I think it would be great if the moon's orbit moved much closer to Earth. How great it would look in the night sky, if, for example, the third part of it would be occupied by a huge glowing sphere, covered with numerous craters and mountain ranges, which can be viewed forever.

I think that the moon has a special influence on people. It has some magnetism in its silence and calmness. Though it is located more than 300 thousand kilometers from us, it still touches our minds with its mysteriousness and calmness. It makes me think that we are not alone in the universe because I cannot think of the moon as a piece of rock. It always had some deep meaning for me, and I will never stop attempting to solve its mystery. As Chang Chiu-Ling once wrote in his brilliant poem: "So I leave my message with the moon/ And turn to my bed, hoping for dreams" (Tuishi and Innes 91).

Works Cited

Tuishi, Heng Tang, and Innes, Herdan. *300 T'ang Poems*. 1st ed. Taipei: Far East Book Co, 1973.
    Print.

Dunbar, Brian. "The Moon." *NASA*. N.p., 2017. www.nasa.gov/moon. 15 Jan. 2017.

Sample 2. Getting Caught in a Summer Shower

Traveling through their lifespans humans encounter millions of situations, both expectable and totally unpredictable. At the age of 13, I went through a memorable experience that caused mixed feelings and provided a valuable life lesson. Everything started in summer camp — the place of my dream, where I was planning to develop as a personality, overcome the difficulties of my character and improve my communicative skills, expanding the circle of my friends. However, as soon as I arrived at my dream-like summer camp, reality knocked on the door of my imagination, transforming my delusional vision of perfect relaxation. Suddenly I realized that I was like a round peg in a square hole, not knowing how to behave appropriately in the company of strangers.

When my peers played the games and gathered into communities, I avoided them and hid away. For some inexplicable reason, I did not trust the people who were surrounding me. I believed that any word or action on my side would lead to deleterious effects and transform everything into an embarrassing situation. Consequently, I preferred staying alone, keeping silent and being unavailable for new acquaintances. Nevertheless, the most significant challenge for me was going to a shared summer shower, as I was too shy, frustrated, and obsessed with the fear of someone seeing me naked.

Because of my unreasonable fear and feeling of abandonment, I started avoiding my peers, going to the dinner beyond the appointed hour and getting up earlier to attend the summer shower ahead of schedule. Consequently, it worked, and I started feeling more self-sustainable, as I did not leave my comfort zone: I just stayed on my own even when being surrounded by hundreds of other people. As a result, I accepted living in the camp, as going to a shared shower became an ordinary morning procedure, not followed by groundless fear or self-distrust, as I was alone.

However, the thirteenth day of living in the campus had dramatically changed my mood. I remember everything as if it happened yesterday: the sun was shining brightly, transforming the corners of my lips into a funny but sincere smile. On my way to a summer shower, I murmured the words from my favorite song, enjoying my independence and limitless comfort. I came into the shared summer shower, regulated the temperature and enjoyed my morning routine, singing the words from my favorite song much louder. Warm water stream lets invigorated me, revealed my energy and provided me with enthusiasm to make this day merely unforgettable. Happiness overwhelmed me, so I sang the words from the most positive songs coming to my mind, such as *I Believe I Can Fly* and *Don't Worry Be Happy*. Suddenly I heard someone's voice, so I turned off the water and looked behind to identify the source of that strange sound, and — I saw two girls, my roommates, singing those awkward songs, laughing and perking their fingers in my face. Having seen these girls, I took on my clothes, came into the room and locked the door to calm down.

Thanks to this experience, I changed significantly. I started exploring the basics of psychology and looking for the reasons of my strange behavior. Having read the reams of published research, I understood that the way I act is affected by psychological phenomena called "toxic shame." I identified the causes of my behavior and moved on toward overcoming this problem. Consequently, I grounded myself in my present, created a vision of the person I want to be, started analyzing my behavior and made the decision to change. Fortunately, I am no longer afraid of shared summer showers, and I am grateful for this funny experience that affected my life. With the help of the stress encountered in summer campus, today I am an active person with a great circle of friends who never stop proving me that my happiness is out of my comfort zone.

Chapter 6. Narrative Essay Writing Guide

If you're an enthusiastic person, you'll definitely enjoy this type of academic writing, as a narrative essay will let your imagination run free and demonstrate the limitless power of your creative potential. But even if you are not exceedingly original, writing a narrative essay will not be a challenge for you, as most humans like sharing their memories, describing invaluable experiences, and, finally, telling different stories. If you are ready to share your emotions with the readers, follow this guide and get immersed in some of the most powerful techniques of effective narration.

What's So Special about a Narrative Essay?

As you might have guessed, the main purpose of each narrative essay is to tell a story. You may inform the reader about a remarkable event from your past, a meeting with a memorable personality, or the ongoing experience that is likely to change your life. Actually, it does not really matter what you are going to tell, as HOW you will tell it is significantly more important.

The majority of students write descriptive essays instead of narrative stories because they do not see the difference between these two types of academic papers. A descriptive essay looks more like an instruction, as it is aimed at explaining how to do something. Additionally, some descriptive essays focus on the external characteristics of the item, explaining in detail how it looks. In contrast to a descriptive essay, the narration is a complete story that has its purpose, beginning, logical connections between the events, clear point of view, the presence of author's personality, and a concise organization of the thought. So do not muddle up these two distinct types of academic writing and go on reading the guideline to explore more specific peculiarities of a narrative essay.

Narrative Essay Writing Structure

Telling a story seems to be an amusingly easy task, as we do it on a regular basis, sharing the emotions with friends or relatives. However, sharing the experiences in academic style is a bit more difficult, as it requires some additional knowledge and skills. In particular, you will have to break your story into patterns, develop a concise organization of the essay, and use some tools of effective personal narration. Here are the most significant of them.

Introduction

The "hook". This element is also called an extraordinary beginning, and using it in a narrative essay is especially important. You may begin your story with a paradoxical fact, relevant quotation, definition, question, or a colorful detail. The main purpose of the "hook" is to grab the attention of your reader from the very beginning of the story to make the audience go through all the personal experiences together with the author.

Setting the scene. Your attention-grabber should be followed by a wide range of visual, acoustic and tactile details. In a narrative essay, it is critically important to set the scene properly: explain where the events take place, who are the main characters, whether they are fictional or real, etc. Also, do not forget to mention whether the experience you are writing about is yours personally or if it belongs to somebody you know. Beginning the story successfully is critically important, as it influences overall perception of the paper.

Thesis statement. In a narrative essay, the thesis statement is significantly different from that in an expository or argument essay. You don't need to introduce your arguments, defend the position, or prove something. Instead, your thesis statement may serve as a beginning of the story: *It was cloudy and hazy when I started my way to green forests.* Additionally, your thesis statement may connect a personal experience with a universal, proving the significance of the topic you write about: *Journeys eliminate the boundaries between different cultures of the world, bringing both hardship and joy to those never-stopping adventurous travelers.* Also, you may use the thesis statement for offering a moral lesson to your audience: *I will never travel alone again, leaving my destiny out of control.* You may find more ways for making your thesis statement effective, just make sure that your thesis serves as the heart of the story that shows your attitude toward the experience you express, and makes the narration unique.

Body Paragraphs

Depict but not tell. It is commonly known that good storytelling is expressive — it is overwhelmed by precise descriptions and sensory details that help the audience to visualize the events illustrated by the author. To make your audience outlive the experiences together with you, use the details related to all five senses: express what you heard, smelled, touched, felt, and saw during the event. Using various sensory details will shorten the distance between you and the audience, establishing a basis for a positive perception of your story.

Support each detail. Using supplementary evidence is required in any type of writing, as it is the most efficient way to make the audience believe you. In a personal narration, your experience represents the deepest source of evidence, which is why you should illustrate the significance of the lesson learned and explain it to the reader.

Emphasize the chronology of the events. Building the storyline in chronological order is the most appropriate so that the readers can understand the logical flow of the events. In case you want to complicate the storyline and destruct the original flow of the events, using the following transitions will help you to put the readers into the picture of the events: during, finally, after, next, later, when.

Keep in touch with the readers. In narrative essays, new paragraphs usually mark the shift from action to reflection or indicate the change in the events. That is why the paragraphs should be linked between one another with transitions. Additionally, it is recommended to repeat the words from the previous paragraph to establish connections between the events being described previously.

Conclusion

Make a powerful inference. In a narrative essay, the conclusion serves as the moral center of the story, as it summarizes everything you have told and provides your story with a significant sense. Due to this, at the end of the story, you should necessarily include a personal reflection or evaluation of the event being described and explain why it is significant for you as the author.

Stages of Writing a Narrative Essay

There is a commonly known five-step model of writing a narrative essay successfully, so let's go through these five stages and find the ways to transform your narrative essay into a polished diamond.

1. Choosing the topic to share. Recreate the memories from childhood, college years, or any other experiences encountered in the first time. Recall the feelings and memories related to those experiences. It will help you to concentrate and pick up an attractive topic for exchange with your audience. Remember that your topic may be any experience, both real and fictional, in your own

life or the experience of your friend or relative. The main purpose is to retell the story comprehensively, supporting it with a wide range of details and attractive word combinations.

2. Draft an outline. Even if you simply retell the story in your essay, you should necessarily prepare an outline that should precisely indicate the plot, the setting, the main characters, the culmination, and the ending of your narration. Remember that writing an amazing story is impossible without strict planning, which is why you should pre-plan each stage of your writing process.

3. Start writing the body paragraphs. Remember that a narrative essay is not the same as any other academic paper. Due to this, you should use as many detail as you can, to provide complete characteristics for personalities, their actions, locations, feelings, etc. The more details you use the better, as it will help the readers to obtain an objective vision of the events being illustrated in your story.

4. Come up with a reasonable conclusion. On this stage of writing, it is necessary to draw a conclusion that will show your attitude to the story, express its significance and help the reader to learn something from your personal experience. This is the final stage of establishing close contact with your readers, which is why you should make it extraordinary and effective, as the last words frequently have the most powerful impact on readers' minds. Consider the most appropriate words to use on this stage.

5. Prepare the paper for submission. After the last words are chosen and written properly, it is time for editing and checking your paper for grammatical and syntactical mistakes, as it does not really matter how unusual and attractive your story is if it contains a considerable amount of mistakes. Also check whether the flow of the events in the paper is logical, and whether the amount of details is sufficient for the readers to understand everything properly.

Guidelines and Tightening Your Essay

The most important thing about writing a narrative essay is providing your readers with a reason to listen to your story and experience this amazing, unique, and unforgettable journey with you. To help you achieve this purpose, here are several tips on how to write brilliant narrations.

1. Take your readers with you. Involving readers in the event is the most important component of effective storytelling, so be sure to recreate the event in an original but simple manner for the readers to understand and remember everything easily. Do not be afraid of expressing your personality through the story, as this is precisely what your audience is expecting from you.

2. Find some generalization to support the story. Equating a personal experience to a universal will provide your paper with a more significant and valuable meaning. For instance, you may connect your story with global problems, related to the state of the environment, gender roles, social issues, poverty in underdeveloped countries, and so on.

3. Link the ideas in a logical manner. Do not forget that the main peculiarity of each successful story is being understandable to the reader. Even if your paper does not include a great number of events, be sure to link them logically. Chronological order is considered to be the most appropriate, which is why using it will not cause any additional problems. Also, do not forget to use transitions: they will help your reader to be in step with the events of the story.

4. Care about accurate structure. Some students believe that a narrative essay provides them with an unlimited space for creativity. Partially, it does, but a narrative essay also has its distinct structure. Due to this, you should start your essay from explaining the prerequisites of choosing the topic, continue by chronological events and supporting details, and finish with proving the significance of the experience described in the paper. Taking into consideration the structure of the body paragraphs, you should remember that each paragraph should be dedicated to one idea only, as otherwise you will blend the events too much and complicate the understanding of the story.

5. Open and close the story in an extraordinary manner. It is highly recommended to begin your essay with a popular quote or meaningful phrase from a movie or book to set the appropriate mood and inspire the reader to follow the events. Besides this, closing the narration effectively is also critically important, as it will prove the significance of your experience and show the value of the story in general. Remember that creativeness is highly appreciated in this type of paper.

6. Avoid wordiness. Long-winded sentences make each paper difficult for perception, which is especially undesirable in a narrative essay.

7. Remember: you are the storyteller. A narrative essay allows the author to use the first-person perspective for retelling the events in a maximally precise manner, so do not be afraid of speaking from your perspective, as it will help you express your own position and establish your authority.

8. Choose a remarkable experience to share with the reader. Selecting an appropriate topic provides you with significant success even before writing. It is much easier to share an unforgettable story than try to write originally about a common and unsurprising life event. Due to this, before writing you should get immersed in the world of your memories, and find a sparkling jewel for your story. Here are some examples of the topics that can become the center of attraction for your future stories.

Narrative Essay Topics

1. Some people hate being challenged, while others enjoy difficulties, perceiving them as opportunities to grow. Tell your story about the greatest challenge and its impact on your mindset.

2. Fear is a natural reaction to a stressful situation, and without fear there would be no bravery. Tell about the most fearful moment of your life and your way of overcoming this unpleasant feeling. Does fear block you or activate all the resources to find the way out of the anxiety? Why does it happen?

3. Living in the modern world can sometimes be tough and even cruel. The golden rule indicates that all people should treat others the way they want to be treated. Though this rule is not always followed, this world still holds a place for kindness. Tell about a situation where you helped somebody and made the world a better place to live in thanks to your rightful action and kindness.

4. Nobody is perfect, and it is definitely a good thing, as some of the greatest world lessons were taken through making a mistake. Tell about the life lesson you took by doing something improperly. What did you feel? What inferences did you make thanks to this experience?

5. Making everybody happy is impossible. Tell about the event or experience when you decided to hurt or disappoint someone, explain the reasons for your actions. If you could come back in time, would you act in the same way?

6. Life is about experience. Experience is about the art of making proper decisions and choices. Tell about a time when you had to choose between two equally important things. How did it affect you? Did you manage to make the right choice?

7. Emotions rule the actions. Tell about the time when your emotions took over the control of your decisions. Do you regret about those reactions? Do you think that emotions are necessary at all?

8. Reputation influences everything. Tell about the times when someone affected your reputation either in a positive or a negative way. What was your reaction to it? Have you ever faced a desire to destroy someone's reputation? If yes, why?

9. Bad habits do not like saying goodbyes, but persistence and practice make miracles. Tell about the times when you gave up bad habits and transformed them into something more beneficial. What helped you to achieve your purpose? Which factors were constantly challenging your self-improvement?

10. Sometimes keeping silent is a better decision than sharing your opinion. Tell about a situation that made you regret about expressing your point of view.

11. Opinions have a great influential power. Tell about personal transformation in the result of misjudgment. Did it break your moral power and influence self-esteem? How to rehabilitate after feelings that awoke as a result of a subjective judgment?

12. People are socially active by nature. Tell about an experience when the world seemed to be an overwhelming place and you wanted to escape from social life to enjoy loneliness. Analyze the causes of such a behavior and provide recommendations for the people who feel something similar.

13. Being talented vs. being lucky. Tell about the event which made you think that talent is unnecessary because fortune is significantly more important. Do you think in the same way today? Do you believe in destiny? If yes, do you think that humans can establish control over their fate?

14. Running from the past is impossible. Tell about your struggles to forget your past. Why do your memories haunt you? Have you resisted successfully? How to get rid of painful or disappointing memories?

15. Sensory feelings are powerful. Scientists believe that scents can become an irreplaceable part of human memories and associations. Share your aromatic associations and the situations when particular scents became a part of your memory.

Mistakes to Avoid While Writing a Narrative Essay

To polish your perfectly great essay, here are some tips on how to avoid the most commonly made mistakes.

1. **Information overload.** Filter all of your thoughts and pre-plan each paragraph before writing, as details are powerful and they really matter, but overwhelming your paper with them will not bring anything positive.

2. **Telling instead of illustrating**. Narrative essay is not a story you tell on a day-to-day basis, as it is creative, enthusiastic, inspiring, coherent, and illustrative. Your narration

should be similar to painting, so do not tell but draw the events to encourage your audience to visualize the events from your text.

3. **Lazy language.** This mistake will transform your extraordinary story in a plain unvarnished tale. To avoid such transformations, select the words thoroughly and do not write in the way you usually speak. Here is the exercise that will help you choose proper words: highlight all the adjectives and nouns in your story and ask yourself: Do these words represent the best choice in this context? If they do not, consider finding better options.

4. **Long sentences.** We have already recommended you to avoid long-winded expressions, but it is worthy to remind this statement and emphasize its importance. Any brilliant story cannot be perceived properly if it is too complicated for comprehension.

5. **Avoiding dialogue.** Writers are afraid of dialogue because they feel responsible for the words put into speech. You should understand that quotes used in the dialogue should not necessarily be direct, as your main purpose is to interpret the dialogue, not to provide its exact reflection. Use dialogue in your writing, as is represents a powerful way to transform your writing into a comprehensive illustration.

6. **Using experience as base material**. Though it sounds a bit strange, it is true. No matter what you are writing, you should go through a transformation of some sort. Your essay will not have any value without some significant message for the readers. Due to this, you should not simply retell your memories, but motivate, encourage, and make your audience feel something similar. Only in that case, your essay can be called successful.

A Narrative Essay Writing Checklist

Introduction

- Have you opened your essay exclusively with the help of a paradoxical fact, relevant quotation, definition, question, or a colorful detail?

- Have you set the scene properly, explaining where the events take place, who the main characters are, if they are fictional or real, and so on?

- Have you included a thesis statement into your introduction? Your thesis may contain the beginning of the story, describe a moral lesson or prove the value of your narration.

Body

- Did you organize your body paragraphs in a logical manner?

- Are the events you describe in body paragraphs linked properly? Did you use transitions to orient the reader in the chronology of the events?

- Have you used sufficient evidence to visualize the events being described? Have you provided the readers with sensory details and properly selected original words?

- Have you linked the paragraphs between one another in a logical manner?

- Have you successfully avoided long sentences and lazy language?

- Did you use first-person narration to eliminate the distance between you and your audience?

- Have you avoided information overload and wordiness?

- Have you chosen an appropriate topic and achieved the purpose of the writing?

- Did you use dialogue to transform a narration into an illustration?

Conclusion

- Have you proved the significance of your story in the conclusion? Have you closed the story in an extraordinary manner?

- Does your story contain some sort of a valuable message for the audience? Does it motivate, encourage empathy or transform the mind of the readers?

- Have you found some generalization to support the story and add some value?

Works Cited

Baker, Jack et al. "Purdue OWL: Narrative Essays." *Purdue Online Writing Lab*, 2013,

owl.english.purdue.edu/owl/resource/685/04/.

"How to Write a Narrative Essay." *AnswerShark.com*, https://answershark.com/writing/essay-

writing/narrative-essay/how-to-write-narrative-essay.html.

"Narrative Essay Writing: Common Mistakes to Avoid." *Bestcustomwriting.com*, 2012,

www.bestcustomwriting.com/blog/essay-writing/narrative-essay-writing-common-

mistakes-to-avoid.

"Narrative Essay Writing." *Essayinfo.com*, http://essayinfo.com/essays/narrative_essay.php.

Paturel, Amy. "Writing a Personal Essay: 8 Common Mistakes to Avoid." *The Write Life*, 2015,

thewritelife.com/writing-a-personal-essay-mistakes/.

"Structure of a Personal Narrative Essay." *Sbcc.edu,* www.sbcc.edu/clrc/files/wl/downloads

/StructureofaPersonalNarrativeEssay.pdf.

"Tips on Writing a Narrative Essay." *Time4writing.com*, www.time4writing.com/writing-

resources/narrative-essays/.

"101 Narrative Essay Topics and Short Story Ideas." *Ereading Worksheets*, 2016,

www.ereadingworksheets.com/writing/narrative-essay-topics-and-story-ideas/.

Sample 1. A Time When I Was Proud of My Nationality

To begin with, it has to be said that as a representative of the Ukrainian nationality, I am lucky to say that I am proud of being a Ukrainian in all senses of this word. As a matter of fact, many people may argue with me: why do you like Ukraine? Aren't you scared living there? And my answer is that although today there are dark times for our country, I still believe that Ukraine will stand up on its feet and thrive soon enough to change our world. Therefore, I am absolutely sure that the time when I am proud of my nationality is now. And thus, I will tell you the reasons of this incredible and fascinating time and place we are now living in.

First of all, it must be underlined that the reason why I like Ukraine and everything Ukrainian is that this country has a great amount of ancient and unique buildings to observe and, therefore, the history to remember. In fact, that is our culture with a lot of bloody battles where Cossacks fought for their independence. Moreover, these buildings and churches are the silhouettes of our past that need to be saved because time is passing by and these buildings are suffering from weather conditions and people's intervention. That's why it has to be highlighted that, although we have a fantastic reflection of the architectural masterpieces, we have to save them and reconstruct all of these monuments for the future of Ukraine.

Secondly, it has to be pointed out that the Ukrainian language is the reason why we have to be proud of our country. As all of us know, the Ukrainian language is the second most melodious language in the world after Italian (8 Interesting Facts About Ukrainian Language 1). Furthermore, it has a great variety of synonyms. Therefore, our language is considered to be the most melodic one to compose and sing songs (8 Interesting Facts About Ukrainian Language 1). However, Catherine Tymkiw, the author of the article "I'm Ukrainian and Proud" and the woman who was born in Ukraine and then settled in Ohio, claims that "Transplanting that Ukrainian identity into Parma, Ohio, was not always easy. And growing up in the Midwest, when I would tell someone I was Ukrainian, I was often met with a confused look. That was followed by, "So, you speak Russian?" (Tymkiw 1). Therefore, as we can see, years ago, if a person lives in Ukraine, people think this person speaks the Russian language, but not Ukrainian. It happened because many people associated Ukraine with the former Soviet Union and thus, all of the people who lived there had to speak Russian. However, in my opinion, nowadays, there are very few people in the world who would ever mix these two languages because of the military conflict in the east of Ukraine. All in all, I truly believe that many tourists and students will come to our country to learn the language soon, but now I am proud of the language I speak.

Thirdly, it must be highlighted that Mother Nature and weather conditions created the fat land for farming. Therefore, many people grow homemade vegetables and fruits. Thus, this is the reason why Ukraine is considered to be a country of harvest. Moreover, the author of the article "Ten Good Reasons To Be Proud of Ukraine" points out that "Until I came to Ukraine I had almost forgotten how a fresh strawberry should taste. I love the seasonality of homegrown foods. It may not come sorted, graded, washed and packed in plastic but who cares when the taste is so real and most of it's fully organic. No, Ukraine is a haven for those who love the taste of real food." (Martin, Nunn 1) Therefore, the farming is one of the main reasons we have to be proud of our country.

Finally, it has to be said that, to my mind, today is the time when I'm proud of my nationality. We have a great variety of ancient buildings, churches, and sceneries that attract a lot of tourists all over the world. Furthermore, we have a melodic language and a fertile land that made this country famous all over the world years ago. So I believe that soon enough, Ukraine will become the first country in the world to visit, and not the country to leave.

Works Cited

Tymkiw, Catherine. "I'm Ukrainian — And Proud." *CNN*. N.p., 20 Feb. 2014.

edition.cnn.com/2014/02/20/opinion/tymkiw-ukrainian-and-proud. Accessed 14 Jan. 2017.

"Ten Good Reasons to Be Proud of Ukraine." *Day.kyiv*. N.p., 15 Jan. 2002.

day.kyiv.ua/en/article/close/ten-good-reasons-be-proud-ukraine. Accessed 14 Jan. 2017.

"8 Interesting Facts About Ukrainian Language." N.p., 2014. Accessed 16 Mar. 2017.

Sample 2. A Time When an Aroma Became Part of My Memory

Smell is considered as one of the five basic human senses. These five senses compose our perception of our surrounding world, feelings, and memories. Strictly speaking, everything we remember is a product of the work of our senses. "Unpleasant and bad smells send pain signals to the brain to warn us of possible danger" ("Why Is Smell Important?"). Therefore, as we can see, smell is not only a pleasant tool for enjoying fragrant flowers or aromatic pizza but also plays a crucial role for our safety. Moreover, the smell gives special shade to each of our memories. For example, when we remember a familiar person, his or her scent is in a special way connected to our emotions and feelings toward this person. If somehow, all the scents had been erased from our memories, most of them would seem distorted.

I have always wondered why, when smelling certain scents, in most cases, blurred memories from my early childhood appear in my mind, but not recent. I used to think that in the first years of our lives, our senses are brighter and sharper, and that is the reason. "Because we encounter most new odors in our youth, smells often call up childhood memories. But we begin making associations between smell and emotion before we're even born" (Dowdey "Smell and Memory"). So, it turns out that we start to smell while in the embryonic stage.

There is a distant recollection from my childhood which I associate with the time an aroma became a part of my memory. Possibly the only scent from my childhood I can remember to this day is the smell of my cradle. What is interesting, I broke most of its parts, being a small child, and my parents had no other choice but to replace it with a new one. But I could not sleep in a new one. Referencing my mother's words, I cried every night, filling the whole apartment with unbearable noise. Initially, my parents soothed themselves with the thought that I would get used to a new cradle in a few days. But I never did. The whining continued, and my father was no longer eager to tolerate this. He went to the attic and gathered all the parts of my old broken cradle. After many hours spent in the garage, he brought my old crib back to life. From that moment, I slept calmly. Of course, with time I stopped being addicted to that scent, but even after so many years I still remember it.

Some time ago, my family and I went to our old house to spend weekends with our relatives who now live there. Even though the house changed its hosts, almost everything remained the same, but the smell. It changed a lot, so I got some kind of confusion. On the one hand, I saw the house where I grew up, but from the other, it had become alien to me. But then I went up to the attic and found my old cradle. I instantly felt its scent and felt an indescribable flood of emotions and memories. It is really amazing how powerful an aroma can be. I decided to take a pillowcase with me in my current apartment and put it in my bed. After that, I never had any problems with sleep.

Works Cited

Dowdey, Sarah. "How Smell Works." *HowStuffWorks*. N.p., 2017. Accessed 15 Jan. 2017.

"Why Is Smell Important?" *Air-aroma.com*. N.p., 2017. Accessed 15 Jan. 2017.

Chapter 7. Compare and Contrast Essay Writing Guide

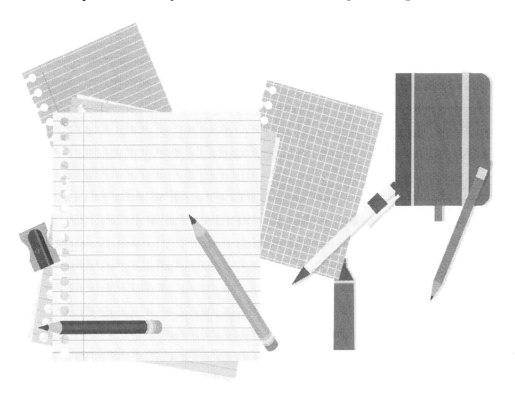

Sometimes compare and contrast essays are paralyzing. You sit in front of the computer screen and simply do not know what to do, and as writer's block attacks you, completing the assignment seems to be impossible, and your self-doubt increases. How to find differences between things that appear to be slightly similar? How to organize your thoughts properly? How to write a good compare and contrast essay and meet the requirements of the academic style? If these questions strike you, do not worry: keep patient, and explore the answers in this guide.

What's So Special About Compare and Contrast Essay Writing?

A compare and contrast essay is a type of academic writing that highlights the ways in which two subjects are similar or different. Comparing the items means finding out the similarities between them while contrasting is focused on the differences. Accordingly, the content of your paper depends on the purpose of writing, as you either compare, or contrast the particular objects and describe the results of it in the paper. Sometimes students are asked to provide both similarities and differences between the items. If you are one of them, keep reading the guide and calm down; here are the answers.

A compare and contrast essay is unique in the manner of explaining your thoughts to the reader, as there are two ways concerning the organization of the ideas in the main body.

1. Block arrangement. Each body paragraph is focused on a particular topic and uses the shared aspect(s) to compare it to the other topic. For instance, if you write about two favorite car models and compare them using several aspects (class, speed, size, etc.), you will have to dedicate the first paragraph to highlighting the aspects related to one car only. The second paragraph will be dedicated to describing the same aspects concerning the other car. In the third paragraph, you may write a conclusion based on the evaluation of two topics and their main points. In this way, using block arrangement, you will concentrate on two different topics and highlight the differences or similarities between them comprehensively.

2. Point-by-point arrangement. Each paragraph is focused on a particular aspect of both topics, which narrows two topics down to patterns. For instance, if you write about the same car models, you will have to dedicate the first paragraph to comparing or contrasting the class of both cars, the second — to their speed, the third — to their size, and so on. In conclusion, you will evaluate the results of the investigation, suggest potential improvements, or recommend a better car model. As you can see, this way of arranging ideas is focused more on the details, while the first one provides a basis for more overall contrast or comparison.

Compare and Contrast Essay Writing Structure

Even if you write the essay on the topic you love and deeply care about, prepare a comprehensive comparative analysis, carry out a deep research, avoid grammar mistakes and never plagiarize, as there is still a possibility of receiving a bad mark. Do you know why? Well, the most common mistake is a failure to choose a convenient structure for organizing your paper properly.

According to two different methods for arranging the ideas in your paper, there are two distinct ways of building your thoughts in the main body. To help you choose a more convenient structure, we provided the examples of both arrangement methods, so evaluate them critically and make a proper choice.

1. Introduction. Introduce two topics that are being contrasted or compared in a short manner. Provide some background, but do not focus on the details, as they are to be highlighted later. Augment your introduction with an effective thesis statement that should present the topic and the argument to the reader. Example: *There is a wide range of benefits provided by Walmart and Safeway, but Safeway is a significantly more appropriate option, as it offers organic produce, ecologically friendly products, and special prices on a great number of goods.*

2a. Main body: block arrangement. Begin each body paragraph with a topic sentence that invites the reader's attention to a particular aspect of the first subject. Topic sentence example: *Walmart is considered to be one of the cheapest supermarkets thanks to a wide range of special offers and sales offered on a regular basis.* Develop a theme based on a topic sentence, and write as many paragraphs as you need to cover all the aspects of the first topic. However, remember that it is not recommended to use more than three aspects. After the first subject is discussed comprehensively, follow the same structure and highlight the second topic.

2b. Main body: point-by-point arrangement. Open each body paragraph with a topic sentence that discusses a certain aspect in both topics, and contrasts and compares the manifestation of the aspect in each topic. Example: *Walmart offers a wide range of special prices and sales, unlike Safeway, whose products consist of chemicals that bring harmful effects to the ecology.* Expand the topic sentence and provide several supporting arguments in each paragraph. Write three paragraphs in general, dedicating each of them to a particular aspect.

3. Conclusion. Your conclusion should necessarily consist of three elements: summarizing the main aspects, providing general evaluation or suggesting future developments, and proving the significance of the topic. Do not repeat any arguments and add any new information, just underline the significance of differences or similarities provided, and show their relevance to your thesis. Example: *With its wide range of special prices, Walmart represents a more appropriate place for shopping than Safeway.*

Stages of Writing a Compare and Contrast Essay

1. Carefully consider the topic. The first step toward an effective compare and contrast essay is carrying out research, reviewing the topics available, and choosing two subjects that are worth deeper investigation. Make sure these subjects have a set of similar or different characteristics to focus on in your investigation.

2. Prepare a list of aspects worthy of comparison. Write down the key differences and similarities between the topics and make a list of them. Use it as a basis for evaluating your topics and developing an argument. Cannot find the similarities and differences independently? Drawing a Venn diagram will help you!

3. Turn the key points into a central statement. Based on the evaluation of two topics, come up with an effective argument and transform it into your thesis sentence. The main mission of your thesis statement is to explain how the subjects chosen relate to each other. Accordingly, you should explain whether they extend, complicate, correct, contradict, corroborate, or debate with one another. The thesis is a central component of the paper, which is why in this sentence you should explain which subject is better or worse and why. Do not forget to introduce the aspects used for evaluating the topics, as they establish the foundation on which your paper will be built. Example: *Most notably, classical music and jazz differ in tempo, manner of playing, audience, and purpose, yet the two have a close connection, as both satisfy human aesthetic needs in high-quality music.*

4. Work on the basis of the paper — the outline. Sketch out the most important points from the list of similarities and differences and your thesis statement. Prepare an outline, as it will form a skeleton of your paper and help you to select the most important aspects for comparison and contrast. Here are two examples of outlines concerning the method of ideas arrangement you choose:

<u>Block Arrangement</u>

Introduction

Main Body

Topic 1 → Aspect 1 + supporting evidence; Aspect 2 + details; Aspect 3 + supporting information.

Topic 2 → Aspect 1 + explanation; Aspect 2 + details; Aspect 3 + supporting evidence.

Conclusion

<u>Point-by-Point Arrangement</u>

Introduction

Main Body

Topic 1 → Aspect 1 + supporting evidence; Topic 2 → Aspect 1 + details.

Topic 1 → Aspect 2 + details; Topic 2 → Aspect 2 + supporting information.

Topic 1 → Aspect 3 + explanation; Topic 2 → Aspect 3 + evidence.

Conclusion

5. Fill in the textual details to augment the outline. After your outline is complete, you should just support each aspect by the evidence from the publications you've read or the results of your personal investigation and experience.

6. Prepare an introduction. It should consist of the hook sentence (extraordinary beginning) and background information on the topic of your choice. Put your thesis statement into the last sentence of the introductory paragraph.

7. Choose the structure of arranging the arguments in the main body. Consider the purpose of the paper and choose the structure that will be the most effective in achieving this purpose. For instance, if you want to investigate the differences and similarities between the topics in general, block arrangement will be more appropriate for you. However, if you want to focus on the details and compare them between two topics, then point-by-point arrangement is the best option.

8. Write body paragraphs according to the chosen structure. Now it's time to return to the outline provided above and just follow all the points mentioned there according to the arrangement type of your choice. Do not forget about topic sentences: they are similarly important in any structure type.

9. Write a conclusion with its structural elements. Significance, evaluation, and summary of the main points — these key components make the concluding sentence of a compare and contrast essay very effective. Make sure you did not miss any of these foundational 'bricks', without which a compare and contrast essay cannot be built successfully.

10. Edit and proofread. Though students often skip this step, we strongly recommend you to dedicate some time and proofread the paper, paying attention to each comma, incorrect or improper word, etc. Omit using colloquial style, as the way you speak in a day-to-day routine must never reflect in your academic papers.

Guidelines and Tightening Your Essay

Sometimes writing a good essay is not enough, as your expectations and resources require something BRILLIANT! To help your expectations become a reality, here are the tips on how to tighten your essay and help it become perfect.

1. Give proper respect to details. This is the main rule of writing an effective compare and contrast essay, as the subject you write about may be what you observe, discuss, or do on a regular basis. You have to dedicate some time and effort to exploring this subject on a deeper level, brainstorming for alternative opinions, and researching. Develop a fresh opinion and defend it as persistently as you can.

2. Clearly define the items you write about. A compare and contrast essay is a very specific type of academic writing, as it requires being maximally precise regarding the definitions you use or the subjects you write about. Make sure your explanations of the topics are broad-based and complete.

3. Use relevant peer-reviewed information. Investigate the subjects deeply before writing and listing their characteristics, as all the data you use should be up-to-date, unbiased, and correct.

4. Care about structure. Do not mix up two distinct methods of idea arrangement, as it is inappropriate for this type of academic writing. Choose either block or point-by-point organization before writing, and follow the model of explaining the ideas suggested in the outline from the Stages of Writing a Compare and Contrast Essay section. Remember that the structure of each paragraph should also be similar, which is why it is worthy to start from the topic sentence, expand it by supporting details and background information, and finish the paragraph by a general conclusion.

5. Consider the needs of the audience. To establish a basis for a positive perception of your paper, it is critically important to divine the needs of your target audience and explore the

information your readers may be interested in. Sketch a list of your audience's interests and include them all in your paper.

6. Prepare a result-oriented outline. Remember that the main criterion for selecting a certain topic is a practical value of the results of your contrast and comparison. Accordingly, while working on your outline, ask yourself the question: Will the results of my investigation have any meaning and practical value for you and your audience? If the answer is "yes," then the topic of your choice is appropriate for this academic paper. But if the answer is "no," you should necessarily change the subject and find a more representative option for a compare and contrast essay.

7. Combine your ideas properly. Follow the arrangement model of your choice, but do not forget about linking the paragraphs between each other in a logical order. Use transitional words and phrases to help the reader avoid getting lost in the maze of the words, as without transitions your essay is going to look like a chaotic flow of unrelated ideas. Here are the examples of transitional words that will help you:

Transitions that show differences: *however, unlike, even though, in contrast, on the contrary, conversely, as well as, at the same time, compared to.*

Transitions that show similarities: *likewise, similarly, in addition, same as, just as, correspondingly, compared to, at the same time, as well as.*

Compare and Contrast Essay Topics

Now you now all the tips for writing an effective compare and contrast essay, so use them in your practice and do your best to make your paper brilliant. However, it is commonly known that without a properly selected topic, all your efforts to write a persuasive compare and contrast paper may come to nothing. Here are the examples of topics that represent a great choice for this type of academic writing.

1. Private vs. public educational institutions: which type provides a better quality of education?

2. Soda water vs. energy drink: compare and contrast their benefits and impacts.

3. Living in the city to living on the farm: compare modern tendencies with earlier times.

4. Being a manager to being a leader: compare and contrast their functions and qualities.

5. Orthodox and Catholic churches: what are the main differences and similarities between their history and theology?

6. Tactical vs. strategic management: which of them is more effective?

7. Greek and Roman art: the main tendencies, differences and similarities in architecture.

8. Google Android vs. iOS: three basic differences and similarities.

9. President Bush vs. President Obama: the key differences in the policy.

10. Online vs. classroom studying: which way of receiving an education is more efficient in modern conditions?

11. Classical music vs. jazz: which music genre is more popular within contemporary listeners?

12. Dried vs. fresh fruit: compare and contrast their nutritional qualities and health benefits.

13. Inner beauty vs. physical: which tendency is better supported by modern advertisements?

14. Traditional vs. extraordinary art: which type of art has more chances to reach and influence the successive generations?

15. Being famous to being rich: what is more important for modern society? Compare priorities of different age groups.

Mistakes to Avoid While Writing a Compare and Contrast Essay

After you've selected a topic, chosen an arrangement type, and prepared an outline, go through this list of the most common mistakes to avoid making them in your essay.

1. Starting the paper without a distinct idea in mind. Too often students begin to write their essays, not understanding the topics comprehensively, and having no clue about the argument they are going to make. This mistake is the most glaring, as it influences the logical organization of the ideas and can leave your paper without any significant results of comparing and contrasting.

2. Trying to connect two organizational methods. In each compare and contrast essay, the structure is the most important component, which is why making this structure illogical cannot be appreciated. Choose either block or point-by-point arrangement before writing not during the process.

3. Failure to select a proper topic. Too often students choose narrow or general subjects for their essays and cannot achieve any valuable results during comparing or contrasting. Make sure that your topic is specific enough to provide you with a broad field for analysis and comparison. Do not choose widely discussed topics, as it would be difficult to make your paper plagiarism-free.

4. Defending a subjective point of view. Even if you are sure that one item is significantly better in comparison with the other, you should use relevant facts to support your position and stay objective.

5. Choosing two equal subjects for comparison. It does not really matter whether your items are similarly good, bad, beneficial, or harmful, but if they really are equal, then exploring which of them is better would be a real challenge, so try to change at least one of them.

6. Forgetting to link the ideas with transitional words. In a compare and contrast essay, connectives carry out very specific functions: they do not only make the flow of ideas logical, but also help the writer to switch the focus from one point to the other. Due to this, the use of transitions is obligatory.

7. Using diagrams and flowcharts in the essay. It seems to be more appropriate to organize the results of your comparison into graphic elements, but actually, it is not, as you are writing an academic paper and should explain everything in a written manner.

However, you can create a flowchart or diagram just for easier navigation through the topics being compared.

8. Ignoring the demands of academic style. Students frequently fail to omit this mistake, as they concentrate on the specific demands of a compare and contrast essay, forgetting about general requirements of academic writing. Remember that your essay should be written in a formal language (without slang and conversational expressions), plagiarism-free, without any grammar, punctuation, and spelling mistakes.

Compare and Contrast Essay Writing Checklist

Introduction

- Have you provided brief background information on the topics being compared or contrasted?

- Is your background information precise and laconic? Does it provide the reader with an accurate understanding of the topics you write about?

- Have you included the thesis statement into the last sentence of the introduction? Does your thesis contain an argument that you defend?

Body

- Have you started each body paragraph with a topic sentence that summarizes a certain idea discussed in the paragraph?

- Have you used evidence to support each idea presented in body paragraphs?

- Have you used transitional words to link the ideas in body paragraphs and between them?

- Have you chosen a proper method for idea arrangement and followed it comprehensively?

- Does your method of organizing ideas correspond to the example provided in the outline?

Conclusion

- Does your conclusion consist of three key components: summary of the main aspects, general evaluation of the topics, and significance of the comparison and contrast?

- Do the results of your investigation have any practical value and meet the requirements of the audience?

Works Cited

Crystal, W. "A Compare and Contrast Essay Outline to Beat Writer's Block." *Kibin Essay Writing Blog*, 2014, https://www.kibin.com/essay-writing-blog/compare-and-contrast-essay outline/.

"How to Write a Compare and Contrast Essay." *Academichelp.net*, 2012, https://academichelp.net/academic-assignments/essay/write-compare-contrast-essay.html.

"How to Write Compare and Contrast Essay." *AnswerShark.com*, https://answershark.com/writing/essay-writing/compare-and-contrast-essay/how-to-write-compare-and-contrast-essay.html.

Kelly, Melissa. "101 Topics for Compare and Contrast Essays." *About.com Education*, 2017, http://712educators.about.com/od/essaysparagraphspapers/a/100-Compare-And-Contrast-Essay-Topics.html.

Saratsiotis, Georgia. "Organizational Patterns for the Comparison/Contrast Essay." *Sjsu.edu*, http://www.sjsu.edu/writingcenter/docs/handouts/Organization_CompareContrast.pdf.

"Step-by-Step Guide to Writing Compare and Contrast Essays." *Study.com*, http://study.com/articles/Step-byStep_Guide_to_Writing_Compare_and_Contrast_Essays.html.

Walk, Kerry. "How to Write a Comparative Analysis." *Writingcenter.Fas.Harvard.edu*, 1998, http://writingcenter.fas.harvard.edu/pages/how-write-comparative-analysis.

"Writing a Compare/Contrast Essay." *Sbcc.edu*, https://www.sbcc.edu/clrc/files/wl/downloads/ WritingaCompareContrastEssay.pdf.

Sample 1. Distinguishing the Social Value of Educated and Experienced People

In recent years, the question of the role and the need of educated people along with experienced ones in the society has been actively debated. Various opinions can be distinguished on whether the mentally trained or experienced nation is the workforce for developing the future of the community.

Primarily, education is defined as obligatory in the modern world. Many people judge other uneducated individuals, considering them as existing on a lower level. In the point of fact, receiving education is essential, as constant progress keeps gaining momentum and in order not to miss it, people have to conform it. The society needs intelligent people, in another case, there will be nobody left to properly develop and rule a country. Hans N. Weiler states that education and knowledge, in particular, is connected with many aspects of social and political life. Regarding knowledge as a political phenomenon, the author correlates it with power as a consequence of obtained knowledge (Weiler 3). From the other hand, practice is significant as well according to its repetitiveness of certain rules and providing the opportunity to analyze the process further. Nevertheless, practice without any educational background cannot be efficient.

The modern education system includes studying a variety of disciplines aimed at making a person think beyond the line. The broad understanding of unconnected subjects, indeed, provokes critical thinking that allows to make assumptions and present arguments while participating in debates or average conversations. Practical skills and great experience obtained in a particular sphere can only establish limited knowledge with no chance to develop. Stephen N. Grimm in his work "Knowledge, Practical Interests, and Rising Tides" claims that education is the most significant way to general perceiving and understanding of the world that, as a result, leads to the personal wisdom (Henderson & Greco 8).

In addition, one of the main reasons why the nation has to be, first of all, educated rather than experienced concerns the duration of the two phenomena. People get older and the practice obtained during the working process will have no sense after a certain age. The primary advantage of getting an education and collecting knowledge is that the skills can last much longer, being of a current interest at any time. Practical skills can be acquired within a relatively short period of time, although the educational process takes the entire life. Moreover, recent researches have illustrated that most of the leading companies in IT and business spheres require educated personnel rather than experienced. The company itself organizes diverse trainings and workshops to help their employees gain practice. However, there is no employer who would like to teach the staff starting from the zero point ("Theoretical Knowledge vs Practical Skills").

In conclusion, comparing the two notions on what the society initially requires, educated or experienced individuals, the answer is for knowledge rather than practice. The time and its requirements are changing dramatically, and in order to be familiar, new people have to improve their brain activity. Practical skills alone cannot provide the opportunity to become an intelligent person who can change the current situation in the world. There is no modern world leader or a businessman without education. Knowledge stays in a person's mind till the last days, and practical skills have its duration. The nation calls for educated people who have a wider picture of the world and can rule it.

Works Cited

Beed, Teresa. "Societal Responsibilities of an Educated Person." 2017,

http://www.newaccountantusa.com/newsFeat/wealthManage.

Henderson, David K and John Greco. *Epistemic Evaluation*. 1st ed., Oxford, United Kingdom,

Oxford University Press, 2015.

"Theoretical Knowledge vs Practical Skills." *The Economic Times*, 2017,

http://economictimes.indiatimes.com/theoretical-knowledge-vs-practical-

skills/slideshow/5922135.cms

Weiler, Hans N. "Theory and Practice: Dichotomies of Knowledge?" Stanford University, 2005,

http://web.stanford.edu/~weiler/Texts05/CIES_paper.pdf.

Sample 2. Travelling to Egypt

The modern era allows studying the world through a variety of ways. There are various sources of information, including books, magazines, the Internet, television, museums, exhibitions, and traveling. In short, there are many possibilities for the expansion of horizons and knowledge. Most people tend to think that it is better to see once than hear a hundred times, especially when we talk about such a unique country as Egypt. However, it is important to remember that the primary task is to formulate precisely the correct idea about the country, its history, culture, society, traditions, and customs. The easiest way that allows to carry out this task is tourism. However, it is possible to create familiarity with the country even without a trip. It is enough to visit a museum that specializes in the study of Egypt. Selection of the best option is a separate aspect, but both ways offer advantages as well as significant differences from each other.

No doubt, any historical artifact or work of art is best to see firsthand. This is the greatest similarity between the trip and the museum as they both provide this issue, but on different scales. Nevertheless, the number of differences is bigger. Most people tend to travel to Egypt primarily to see such incredible touristic places as the Pyramids or Sphinx, which is undoubtedly a great experience. Another advantage of tourism is full contact created in society (Burns, Peter et al.). In the museum, we can see the historical place partly. Meanwhile, being in Egypt means the involvement in the society, culture, language and traditions. So if the museum is the scene, then the trip is the vast background. Tourism also provides excellent recreational abilities, and this is one of the primary reasons that makes people travel.

However, not everyone can travel a lot around the world. Usually, museums hold second place among travel priorities. Moreover, a visit to the museum can be tedious and even unpleasant in the case of the absence of proper preparation or violation of the rules of the museum. This issue distinguishes the exhibition from tourism because usually a tourist trip has fewer rules and limitations. However, an advantage of the museum is the ability to get, at the same time, intellectual joy and aesthetic pleasure. When it comes to an exhibition related to a particular historical period or place, it would be wise to learn about the proposed exhibits before the visit to the museum. Thus, the effectiveness of the visit will be much higher. In general, museums and exhibitions involve greater intellectual potential and benefits than a visit to the country, since it is possible to find things and people that specialize in them, and they can provide more information. Also, the museum can show previously unknown aspects of the lives of ordinary people, such as everyday item and clothes. Another characteristic feature is the cooperation with technologies. Today, in the modern digital age, people have the opportunity to visit some of the most famous museums in the world from the comfort of their home. For example, the Louvre offers free online tours, during which people can see some of the most famous and popular exhibits — in particular, the Egyptian relics (Carreras, Cèsar, and Federica Mancini). Therefore, museums provide more intellectual, comfortable and available ways to learn about Egypt.

To sum up, the question of choice depends on people's desires and possibilities. However, it is possible to note that tourism has greater experience making abilities and recreation base while museum suits for people with intellectual aims and those who look for a comfortable way to communicate with Egypt culture and history.

Works Cited

Burns, Peter et al. *Tourism and Visual Culture*. 1st ed., Cambridge, Mass., CAB International, 2010.

Carreras, Cèsar and Federica Mancini. "A Story of Great Expectations: Past and Present of

Online/Virtual Exhibitions." *DESIDOC Journal of Library & Information Technology*, vol 34,

no. 2, 2014, pp. 87-96. *Defence Scientific Information and Documentation Centre*,

doi:10.14429/djlit.34.6749.

Final Thoughts

Thanks for reading our book. We do hope you found it useful, and that it will be your table-book during the years of study. Our writers tried to make it as simple as possible for you to master the art of essay writing with ease, and to avoid the most common mistakes.

"Essay Becomes Easy. Part I" may be useful both for high school beginners and experienced university students. We've presented the best examples, detailed guides and useful topics to make our book practical and helpful.

Try to write your next essay with our book and you will definitely achieve success.

Made in the USA
Monee, IL
26 January 2023

26139134R00072